PRAISE F...
DISCOVER YOUR TRUE WORTH

"When the Lord gave me the message *Woman, Thou Art Loosed* some twenty-five years ago, I had no idea how it would grow, resonate, and help unravel the tangled lives of countless women around the globe. I see the message in *Discover Your True Worth* as a similar handbook, one that will guide women who are on the journey to becoming all that God created them to be and to making a difference in every facet of life and every sphere of influence. Congratulations to Lindsay Roberts for being a woman who allows the many aspects of her life to help other women find their path for the journey ahead of them."

—BISHOP T.D. JAKES, *NEW YORK TIMES* BESTSELLING AUTHOR

"As a child of God, we must understand our worth. Lindsay encourages us to discover who we are, who we are made in the image of, and what our useful purpose is! So many of us, myself included, have struggled to find our place in the 'big scheme of things' because we get sidetracked by our failures and mistakes. We think there's no way God could use a broken vessel like me in His mighty work. That's what Lindsay shows us: His power is made perfect in our weakness, aka misfortunes, mistakes, and mishaps. Come on this journey with Lindsay to discover why God made you HIS HEIR! He loved you so much, He stretched out His arms and died just for you."

—MISS KAY ROBERTSON, MATRIARCH OF THE ROBERTSON
FAMILY, AUTHOR, SPEAKER, FLAWED BUT FAVORED

"I believe this book must get into the hands of every woman currently in ministry and every woman who feels called to serve God in any way. It is provocative, challenging, and personal. Wait until you get to the chapter 'Becoming a Woman of Faith.' Your life may never be the same."

—KEVIN ADELL, CEO, THE WORD NETWORK

"*Discover Your True Worth* is not just a book, it's a concept dear to Lindsay's heart. I have personally witnessed the transformation God has brought to her life over our many years of friendship and believe she is uniquely qualified to help others find the value God has placed in them. Her great faith in God and her great love for women are evident in every page of this important book. Each chapter is designed as a step on the journey toward living every day in the understanding of your true worth and value as God sees you. As you read about the journeys Lindsay and others have taken, I pray you will realize just how much God values you."

—MARILYN HICKEY, INTERNATIONAL BIBLE
TEACHER, AUTHOR, TELEVISION HOST

"*Discover Your True Worth* can be a powerful inspiration to all who choose to dwell in its pages! We are particularly blessed by the chapter 'Welcome to the Un-convention,' as both of our lives have been unconventional. We walked on the dark side of life before we heard God calling our names. Once we ran to Him, we realized how powerfully God can use unconventional people. This book will be a comfort and a source of strength to all who have suffered and long to see God turn their pain into a beautiful purpose. We pray this book will touch and transform women all over the world as they celebrate and embrace who they were created to be."

—DUANE "DOG THE BOUNTY HUNTER" AND FRANCIE CHAPMAN,
UNCONVENTIONAL MESSENGERS FOR JESUS' SAKE

"'What is my worth?' This is a question I hear often and a topic requested by the viewers of *Joni Table Talk*. In *Discover Your True Worth*, Lindsay Roberts walks readers through the Bible, telling the story of women who, even in uncertainty, discovered their true identity in what God had destined them to accomplish. I highly recommend this engaging book to guide you in discovering your true worth."

—JONI LAMB, COFOUNDER, DAYSTAR TELEVISION NETWORK

"This book is wonderful and powerfully anointed. I personally know the 'behind the scenes' battles and great victories that Lindsay has fought and won by faith. She learned the things she has written about from the Word of God and from her experiences. *Discover Your True Worth* is a must-read, not only for women but for men as well."

—KENNETH COPELAND, AUTHOR; FOUNDER OF KENNETH
COPELAND MINISTRIES AND THE VICTORY NETWORK

"*Discover Your True Worth* will empower you to live an unconventional life because we serve an unconventional God. Through stories of ordinary women in the Bible, Lindsay Roberts shows you how to draw the value and worth out of your life and be all God called you to be. I highly recommend this book!"

—LISA OSTEEN COMES, ASSOCIATE PASTOR, LAKEWOOD
CHURCH, HOUSTON; AUTHOR, *IT'S ON THE WAY*

"Lindsay Roberts is a valuable treasure who shines brilliantly through the pages of her book *Discover Your True Worth*. Lindsay has boldly embraced her mandate to help women prepare to take their rightful place and come to the forefront of life. Her book shatters the mold of the way the world—and even some in the church—expect women to be and reveals how valuable women are to God and to others."

—CATHY DUPLANTIS, JESSE DUPLANTIS MINISTRIES;
COFOUNDER, THE COVENANT CHURCH

"This is a NOW book for women. As a woman of faith, Lindsay Roberts shares how she applies God's Word to her life and family in many situations. She relates the heartache she experienced during many years of ministry. Just as the women of faith mentioned in the Bible impacted their nations centuries ago, Lindsay reminds women today that they can do the same. This book is designed to encourage and strengthen you to become the woman of God that He has called you to be."

—REV. MARGARET COURT AC, MBE, SENIOR PASTOR—VICTORY LIFE
CENTRE INC., PERTH, WESTERN AUSTRALIA; PRESIDENT, VICTORY
LIFE INTERNATIONAL BIBLE TRAINING CENTRE INC; PRESIDENT,
VLCS INC (T/A MARGARET COURT COMMUNITY OUTREACH)

"I believe this book can completely transform your self-worth and should be required reading for every woman who longs to believe in her true worth and live the life she's worth living. Lindsay has such a brilliant and fun way of bringing you into the real-life events of women, just like you and me, who could have spent their lives under a defeated self-image. I am confident that, after diving into their relatable stories, you can hold your head up high, pull your shoulders back, and embrace a new identity in Christ."

—TERRI SAVELLE FOY, AUTHOR, TELEVISION HOST

"We appreciate Lindsay's honest approach and transparency as she shares real-life stories and examples in this book. During a time when many women are struggling in different ways, *Discover Your True Worth* can offer them guidance in becoming all they are meant to be. We enjoyed reading this book and highly recommend it."

—DR. DON AND MARY COLBERT, *NEW YORK TIMES* BESTSELLING COAUTHORS

"In a time when many people seek their sense of worth from the number of 'followers' on social media, Lindsay Roberts has written what I believe to be a life-altering book that shifts the focus to what is truly important. She unveils through amazing stories and wisdom that God's opinion of you makes other people's opinions secondary. I believe this book to be a guide to true greatness. Sometimes we are one generation away from eternal change, and I feel this book can bring that kind of change to women everywhere and truly transform a person, a family, and even a generation desperate for approval."

—TIM STOREY, AUTHOR, SPEAKER, AND LIFE COACH

DISCOVER *YOUR* TRUE WORTH

DISCOVER *YOUR* TRUE WORTH

Becoming the Woman God
Created You to Be

LINDSAY ROBERTS

EMANATE
BOOKS

Published in Nashville, Tennessee, by Emanate Books, an imprint of Thomas Nelson. Emanate Books and Thomas Nelson are registered trademarks of HarperCollins Christian Publishing, Inc.

Unless otherwise noted, Scripture quotations are taken from the New King James Version®. Copyright © 1982 by Thomas Nelson. Used by permission. All rights reserved.

Scripture quotations marked AMPC are taken from the Amplified® Bible (AMPC). Copyright © 1954, 1958, 1962, 1964, 1965, 1987 by The Lockman Foundation Used by permission. www.Lockman.org.

Scripture quotations marked ESV are taken from the ESV® Bible (The Holy Bible, English Standard Version®). Copyright © 2001 by Crossway, a publishing ministry of Good News Publishers. Used by permission. All rights reserved.

Scripture quotations marked KJV are taken from the King James Version. Public domain.

Scripture quotations marked THE MESSAGE are taken from *THE MESSAGE*. Copyright © 1993, 2002, 2018 by Eugene H. Peterson. Used by permission of NavPress. All rights reserved. Represented by Tyndale House Publishers, Inc.

Scripture quotations marked NIV are taken from The Holy Bible, New International Version®, NIV®. Copyright © 1973, 1978, 1984, 2011 by Biblica, Inc.® Used by permission of Zondervan. All rights reserved worldwide. www.Zondervan.com. The "NIV" and "New International Version" are trademarks registered in the United States Patent and Trademark Office by Biblica, Inc.®

Scripture quotations marked NLT are taken from the Holy Bible, New Living Translation. © 1996, 2004, 2015 by Tyndale House Foundation. Used by permission of Tyndale House Publishers, Inc., Carol Stream, Illinois 60188. All rights reserved.

Any internet addresses, phone numbers, or company or product information printed in this book are offered as a resource and are not intended in any way to be or to imply an endorsement by Thomas Nelson, nor does Thomas Nelson vouch for the existence, content, or services of these sites, phone numbers, companies, or products beyond the life of this book.

ISBN 978-0-7852-9075-9 (eBook)
ISBN 978-0-7852-9074-2 (TP)

Library of Congress Cataloging-in-Publication Data

Names: Roberts, Lindsay, author.
Title: Discover your true worth: becoming the woman God created you to be / Lindsay Roberts.
Description: Nashville: Emanate Books, [2022] | Summary: "Lindsay Roberts helps women understand that no matter their fears, failures, hurts, or hopes, they can be set free to discover their true worth in Christ and become the women God created them to be"-- Provided by publisher.
Identifiers: LCCN 2021043685 (print) | LCCN 2021043686 (ebook) | ISBN 9780785290742 (tp) | ISBN 9780785290759 (ebook)
Subjects: LCSH: Christian women--Religious life. | Self-esteem in women--Religious aspects--Christianity. | Identity (Psychology)--Religious aspects--Christianity.
Classification: LCC BV4527 .R583 2022 (print) | LCC BV4527 (ebook) | DDC 248.8/43--dc23
LC record available at https://lccn.loc.gov/2021043685
LC ebook record available at https://lccn.loc.gov/2021043686

Printed in the United States of America
22 23 24 25 26 LSC 10 9 8 7 6 5 4 3 2 1

*To Jordan and Olivia and Chloe, my gifts from God,
the three most wonderful girls I will ever know. You
are the inspiration behind this book, and I pray
you will always know your true worth in God.*

*To Richard, for always being there for me with your
constant love, encouragement, and support (and for
typing this manuscript over and over and over . . .)*

*And to Oral and Evelyn Roberts, now part of the
great cloud of witnesses cheering us on. Without your
insight and example, this book would not exist.*

CONTENTS

CONTENTS

INTRODUCTION

Whole.
Healed.
Strong.
Secure.
Unconditionally, infinitely loved by God.
A woman of immeasurable worth, sure of who she is in Christ.

These are words I think of when I think of you. I have an overwhelming desire to see women whole and healed in every area of their lives so they will know the joy of discovering their true worth and understand how valuable they are to God. Maybe these words represent what you desire for yourself and hope to find through this book. I have written it with the prayer that you will indeed realize and experience those things in the depths of your soul. I would encourage you, before you read any further, to ask the Holy Spirit to minister to you in uniquely personal, powerful ways.

Before I continue, let me say that I know many women have yearned for a sense of worth, for healing, and for wholeness for many years—so long that they may wonder if they will ever receive it. Maybe you are one of them. If your faith seems shaky but your longing is deep, I believe you can realize everything you long for. I am absolutely convinced that the Lord desires to fill your life with strength, purpose, joy, and a deep awareness of how special and valuable you are.

I invite you—whether you have great faith or only a tiny bit of belief that God will come through for you—to join your faith with mine and believe with me that God will do something wonderful in your life through the pages of this book. You may find it interesting to know that my story of discovering my true worth began way back in 1959.

Though I now host a national television program, I started out as a shy, studious brainiac in Michigan. My life has been an unusual journey for sure. I was born in December 1955, and unlike many little girls, many of my earliest memories involve baseball. Yes, I'm a lifelong Major League Baseball fan, and the Detroit Tigers have always been my team. In the house where I grew up, Tiger baseball seemed almost as important as things like schoolwork. Names like Mickey Mantle, Al Kaline, and Denny McLain filled our conversations so often that I actually thought they were my relatives.

As a child, my world did not extend beyond Flint and Detroit, Michigan, and being the daughter of a successful car dealer. And as a big Tigers fan, I got my first Tiger baseball ring when I was two or three years old, or so I was told. By the time I could read and write, I was learning how to keep a box score, collecting baseball cards, writing down every player's name, and recording any baseball statistic I could read. As far back as I can remember, if the Tigers played at home, I tried my best to be there.

But on July 6, 1959, at 4:20 p.m., there was no baseball game at Tiger Stadium. One of the biggest events in town that night did not include sports celebrities, just a faith-filled preacher.

That summer afternoon, a remarkable man sat quietly in a hotel room just a short distance from the stadium, preparing to preach to those who would listen and then to do what he loved most on earth: to pray for the sick and lead people to Jesus.

That man was a healing evangelist from Tulsa, Oklahoma, and before he entered the tent to speak to approximately twelve thousand people gathered inside and a thousand more standing outside, he penned this fervent prayer:

MY PRAYER TODAY

Detroit, Michigan

July 6, 1959

4:20 p.m.

Make me like you, Jesus. Increase my faith.

Fill me with more understanding, more compassion. Let me act wisely and move in God's will.

Toughen me to take anything the devil sends my way.

To suffer it with my head up.

To continue my ministry as usual.

To love everyone.

To obey God with all my heart.

God bless and deliver the people of my generation.

Whatever happens to me, deliver the people.

In the name of Jesus of

Nazareth, amen.

There were no RBIs (runs batted in) in Detroit that day. No walks, no balls, no stolen bases, no home runs, no strikeouts, no kicking dirt at the umpire. There was just a solitary man sitting in the silence of a hotel room talking to God—a man called by God, who would faithfully serve Him until he went to heaven at age ninety-one and who would hold a healing crusade that night in an enormous tent pitched not far from the stadium. That man, a stranger to my world in 1959, years later became my father-in-law, Oral Roberts.

Oral's ministry journey was not easy, but despite all the controversy he faced, all the ridicule he endured, and everything he went through, he knew who he was and what he was to do for God. And about forty years after that day in Detroit, my father-in-law poured into me what he believed—and what I now truly believe—was a mandate from God to help women discover who they are in Christ and establish them in their powerful identity in Him.

I knew when Oral called my husband, Richard, and me to his home in California because he "had an idea," that he had something significant to share. At the time, he was nearing his eighty-eighth birthday, and we had already planned to travel to California to celebrate. I promised him that when we arrived, I would be ready to jump into his newest project.

That day we celebrated his birthday, enjoyed balloons, shared a meal, and took a few family pictures. But I could tell something unusual was weighing on his mind. As the celebration began to settle down, Oral didn't settle down at all. He was restless, almost anxious. He was ready to work, even though the room was full of people.

Once the room began to clear, he told me he had a recurring dream concerning Luke 8 and "women of substance." The Merriam-Webster online dictionary defines *substance* as "essential nature" and "a fundamental or characteristic part or quality." It also describes *substance* as "material possessions: property."[1] According to Strong's online definition, *substance* in Luke 8 is used to describe "things which one possesses."[2] I believe Oral's message to me about women of substance embodied all of this.

As he explained it to me, I saw the message as this: Women must discover who we are and what we are made of in order to move forward in all God wants us to become. We must begin to understand our worth (we will never know it fully on this side of heaven) and see how valuable we are *in* God and *to* God.

In this book, when I use the terms *worth*, *true* worth, or *worth* and *value*, I am referring to our worth as spiritual worth God sees in us. At the core of this revelation was that now is the season for women to prepare to come to the forefront of life—in business, in the church, in our families, and in every area of society—to take our rightful places as God planned from the time He formed the very first woman, Eve, in the garden of Eden.

Oral knew, through the power of God and divine revelation, that women must see ourselves according to who we are in Christ. And when we do, a new day will dawn for us spiritually, physically, financially, emotionally, relationally (in our marriages, families, and friendships), in the workplace, in the marketplace, and in all aspects of life.

Before I continue the story of my remarkable conversation with Oral that day, let me clarify: this revelation is not to push men out of their rightful place in God's design, but for women to be strong enough and spiritual enough to take the place God has designed for them. Oral viewed women as well able to do all God calls them to do with excellence, with anointing, with strength, and with great joy. That's a view I share. Women who know their worth in God are excellent, anointed, strong, filled with joy, and used mightily by God. They know the satisfaction of serving Him from a place of wholeness and health in spirit, soul, and body.

Now, back to what happened in California after Oral's birthday celebration. Having shared his understanding of God's heart for women, Oral then opened his Bible, as he always did, and walked me through Luke 8.

Many people read Luke 8 and focus on the parable of the sower (Luke 8:4–8), but that's not what Oral wanted to highlight. His attention was fixed on verses 1–3, a short story about Mary Magdalene, Joanna, and Susanna—three seemingly unknown or insignificant women, yet who were so important to Jesus that He mentioned them by name. Oral went on to talk about the emphasis Jesus placed on women and the genuine value He recognized in them. He explained their extreme uniqueness and how Jesus wanted to pull off the oddity of the ages by drawing women together in amazing unity for the purposes of His kingdom. He spoke to me of the enormous trust Jesus placed in women and pointed out that they were so significant that God trusted them to be there for Jesus at His birth, at His death, and at His resurrection.

During this unusual conversation, I began to discover Oral's heart's desire: he felt that in the next cohesive move toward Jesus' return, women would play a very important, strategic role, just as they did in Luke 8. His passion at the time of his eighty-eighth birthday was to impart to me what God was imparting to him about women becoming a strong unit, a powerful force for

God, and an important part of what He needs to fulfill His plan in this day to set the stage for His Son's soon return. Women have always been there to set the stage and prepare the way for Jesus, just as Mary Magdalene, Joanna, and Susanna set the stage and prepared the atmosphere for one of Jesus' greatest teachings.

As Oral shared the dreams and the revelation God had given him, he told me he felt in his heart that this revelation was a mandate for me, not for him. It was something I must listen to and carry out as God would lead me. He was committed to depositing this in me and mandating me to carry it forth, sharing it with as many women as possible—and that's how this book came to be.

This book is not for the "perfect" Bible study girl who wakes before dawn to read Proverbs 31 and ends each day with the determination of Scarlett O'Hara. While Proverbs 31 is an amazing source of spiritual wisdom and knowledge (I've dedicated a major portion of chapter 4 to the Proverbs 31 woman), it is not intended to pressure us to strive for some kind of biblical perfection. Frankly, I'm not sure the "perfect woman" exists. I am convinced, however, that we can do our best and learn to grow from our life experiences, whether they are good or bad, right or wrong. I'm also certain that regardless of our shortcomings, mistakes, and regrets (we all have them), we are more valuable than we have ever imagined.

We women can be hard on ourselves when we don't feel we're getting everything "right." To get to the place where we feel "right," we sometimes have to go through a lot of wrong. I know that feeling, because I've been that woman and I still am that woman. It makes me who I am. So if you've ever cried, feared, fallen, risked, failed, prayed, hoped, loved, lost, forgiven, held on, or walked away; if you've ever been discouraged or perplexed or felt frozen in time—somewhere between heaven and earth or in the middle of nowhere—then this is the book for you. It's for women like you and me, women of worth who are asking God to draw our substance out of us and bring it to the forefront so we can be all He has called us to be.

You and I are on a journey of allowing the Holy Spirit to draw out our true substance—that which God has placed inside of us for His purposes, to help fulfill His plan—and to live from a place of humbly recognizing our worth. I hope this book will be a companion for you on this journey, a place where you will find lessons, advice, and truth that empower you to walk forward confidently and well. You'll also find in these pages stories about some amazing women in the Bible who have characteristics, imperfections, and challenges perhaps just like yours.

As you read the following pages, remember that a journey of a thousand miles begins with one step. The journey toward the woman God made you to be begins with exactly who and where you are right now, in this very moment. That's what Jesus works with—all the mess and confusion, stubbornness, sweetness, kindness, persistence, exhaustion, and everything else you have to offer Him—the good, the bad, the happy, the sad, the pretty, the ugly, the whatever. Whatever you have and whoever you are is God's raw material as He prepares to shape you into the woman God envisioned when He created you.

My prayer is that as you read, you will be encouraged, strengthened, inspired, and set free to become all and do all that God has in His heart for you to be and do.

WELCOME TO THE UN-CONVENTION

Perhaps you—like the women in the Bible, like many women in general, and like me—have found that your journey through life feels unconventional. It may not be what you envisioned as a little girl. You may have had days when trying to live your dreams seemed more like starring in a comedy of errors. You've probably had to find your own path, which involved a good deal of stumbling along the way. You may have made silly mistakes and even costly mistakes. Maybe you have survived heartbreak that made you wonder if you could keep going or if God could ever use you. I've heard that there is part of God's heart that you cannot know unless you have suffered.

> There is part of God's heart that you cannot know unless you have suffered.

Maybe your sufferings—or even your mistakes—have played out in the public eye, or maybe you never told a soul other than God. Either way, if you are like most women I've encountered in more than thirty-five years of ministry, you have felt unworthy of God's blessing at some point and wondered if He could or would redeem the confusing or painful situations in your life.

The good news is that God didn't create you to stumble through your days or to soldier through a mediocre existence. And yes, He absolutely wants to use you and redeem your life. The Bible explains that He is in the business of renewal. Romans 12:2 says, "Do not conform to the pattern of this world, but be transformed by the renewing of your mind" (NIV). First Corinthians 2:16 says, "We have the mind of Christ." So, when we see things with a mind that's been renewed to think as Christ thinks, while you may look in the mirror and see a sinner, He sees an amazing work in progress. Where you see a mess, He sees a miracle. Where you feel bad, sad, weird, freakish, different, quirky, inauthentic, or just plain ugly on the inside or out, He sees true beauty.

When you think, *I've messed up too many times*, He thinks, *She is about to understand that she needs Me.*

When you think, *God can't possibly want to look at me. I've made too many bad decisions*, He thinks, *There she is! My friend! I can't wait for her to look to Me for help and discover that we have so much to accomplish together!*

For me, Lindsay Roberts, the truth of the Bible is that God is in the business of the unconventional.

The definition of *unconventional* is "not based on or conforming to what is generally done or believed."[1] God has actually used unconventional people and circumstances from the very beginning.

Think about Adam. Now *there* was someone who did not conform to what was generally done—a human being formed of dust, given life by the breath of God (Genesis 2:7).

> The truth of the Bible is that God is in the business of the unconventional.

Remember what happened at the Red Sea, when God rolled it back and allowed His people to walk to freedom on dry ground (Exodus 14:21–22)? That was unconventional.

Consider the time the sun stood still so God could give His people a seemingly impossible victory over their enemies (Joshua 10:12–14). That had never happened before and hasn't happened since. Unconventional.

Perhaps the story of Jesus is the most unconventional of all:

- He was born of a virgin (Matthew 1:18–23).
- He was a King, yet He was born in a manger (Luke 2:6–7).
- He came to reign but spent His time serving everyone around Him (Matthew 2:2; 20:28).
- He lived like a saint but walked among sinners (Mark 2:17; John 1:14).
- He ministered on the streets but went to heaven to prepare dwelling places for us (John 14:2).
- He was strong, yet He loved the weak (Romans 5:6).
- He said that to gain, we must first give (Luke 6:38).
- He ultimately died so that we could live (John 3:16).
- He was a man so unconventional that even the grave could not hold Him (Matthew 28:7)!

That's Jesus, the host of this un-convention.

Jesus knows all about our unconventionality. He understands that we all face different obstacles, messes, and challenges. I offer this 1-2-3 pattern to use each time you encounter one:

1. Get up.
2. Try again.
3. Keep moving forward.

To reach number 3, a person must first go through numbers 1 and 2—and 1 and 2 might be messy. But sometimes that's the way it is on our paths to becoming women God can use. It's definitely that way on the journey of learning who we are and who God is.

Life is a series of learning experiences. Not all of it is good or perfect. If you have attended a church or a Bible study that has made you feel you had to be perfect or that you were not worthy to be called a woman of God, I am sorry. God does not expect you to be perfect. I do believe He wants you to be excellent, but He knows full well that you will never achieve perfection.

In Daniel 5:12 we read that Daniel had "an excellent spirit" but not that Daniel was perfect. A spirit of excellence means doing things to the very best of our ability in the best way possible and not slacking off. As we do things as unto God, we are to do them with excellence in His name and in His honor as best we can. When we try to be perfect, we do things in our own way only to see how great we can do them. The huge difference

> The huge difference between excellence and perfectionism is who gets the glory.

between excellence and perfectionism is who gets the glory. In excellence, God gets the glory, but in perfectionism, we are looking to make sure we've done a job that satisfies ourselves or the people around us. That's all about self as opposed to all about God. The intended recipient of the results of excellence is God. The intended recipients of the outcome of perfectionism may be ourselves, the people around us, or a combination of both.

I know about perfectionism. Growing up, I so desperately wanted to please people and thought I could do it only by being perfect. I felt terrible if I scored a 98 out of 100 on an assignment or test because it was so close but not perfect. By the time I was in the third grade, I started having ulcers.

Being a perfectionist and a people pleaser rather than a God pleaser is not God's best. No one can please 100 percent of the people around them 100 percent of the time, and you can make yourself sick trying. But as you reach for excellence, as Daniel did (Daniel 6:3), to glorify God by simply doing your best and giving Him your best, the result is very different from that of perfectionism. In my case, I felt God's love and appreciation and sweet smile. And in my case, it was ulcer-free.

The only perfect One on earth was Jesus. Period. Ever. So we need to delete from our thinking the need to be perfect. However, the good news is that Philippians 3:14 says we can get up and "press toward the goal for the prize of the upward call of God in Christ Jesus." We can trade in a perfectionistic tendency for an excellent spirit, knowing that we are works in progress and that God loves us just as we are. He will continue to help us grow, change, and mature—but He loves us right where we are today.

> The only perfect One on earth was Jesus. Period.

WHO AM I WITHOUT MY LIPSTICK?

My perfectionistic tendencies suffered a brutal blow not long after I joined the Roberts family. Use your imagination and go with me on a trip I made to the dentist after marrying Richard in 1980. Picture me all dressed up, because after the appointment I was having lunch with the big cheese, Oral Roberts, Richard's dad.

In addition to lunch with "O. R." and a few others, this big lunch also included my very-well-put-together new mother-in-law, Evelyn Roberts. The purpose of the lunch was to chat about my role in the ministry. *God, help me*, I thought. Being on television, being up front, and being in the so-called limelight was never my intent.

When I met Richard, I was in law school, an introverted bookworm who was more comfortable deep inside my thoughts than anywhere else. As far as I was concerned, I was perfectly placed alphabetically in the last row of the classroom. On school days, I went to that last row, sat in the back, and wouldn't speak unless spoken to. This worked for me. The idea that I could be pulled from that safe spot in the back to the front of a world-renowned ministry terrified me.

So, just to be sure things went as planned on the day of the lunch meeting, I was up early, hair-doed, makeupped, and ready to face the great unknown. I was about to head off into uncharted waters, and I wanted to be prepared. If I looked the part, maybe I could act the part, right?

But first things first. My teeth. Easy-peasy. No problem. At least that's what I figured when I sat down in the dentist's chair, ready to check the appointment off my list and head to my "destiny in the ministry" lunch. A simple checkup and I'd be on my way. But oh, how wrong I was.

I was sitting in the chair when in walked a precious lady holding a tissue. My mind was somewhere else completely, but then she told me to "take it off." I wasn't sure what she meant until the tissue came toward my face—and then I knew. She wanted me to take off all my lipstick and remove any makeup from the surrounding area, where I had carefully piled on layers of "perfect coverage." *Oh, dear Lord, no. No. No. NO,* I thought. Knowing that my father-in-law's take on makeup was "Pile it on. Any old barn could use a good coat of paint," I was absolutely terrified.

There I sat, watching my face, which I had strategically and carefully created (maybe even artistically), turn into nothing more than a smudge on a tissue as it went right into the trash. But it wasn't all gone, I had to admit. Just from the cheeks down, with a nice, clean dividing line on my face. It was just like the "before and after" on a makeup commercial, but instead of a face divided from left to right, mine was divided horizontally, with my nose as the obvious point of division.

To make matters worse, the appointment was longer than expected. That was a problem because Oral and Evelyn were always on time.

When I finished at the dentist office and sprinted out to my car, I looked in the mirror and gasped. I couldn't laugh because it wasn't funny, but I couldn't cry because my eye makeup was all the makeup left on my face. I was *not* losing my last quadrant of face paint. But with no time to stop and no "repair kit" in the car, I was very low on options. So, what now? Seriously, what now?

The only thing I could think of, when all else fails—*schmear.* Yep, schmear! The famous "Granny spits to wipe it off your face" technique. Except in my case it was the "spit on your finger and wipe it around" technique—in the driver's seat of my car. So, I spit. I schmeared. I gathered my courage, and I made a choice.

What if my makeup was gone? What if I lost that sense of security about meeting with Oral and Evelyn Roberts for lunch? I was going in!

I walked into the restaurant wearing only half the makeup I had planned. I met my newfound fate head-on. I laughed, I joked, and I talked with boldness as I faced the big question, *Who am I without my lipstick?*

During that lunch, I quickly decided that with or without makeup, I was who God made me to be—in His image and for His purpose.

Did I need some tweaking? Yes. Did I need some help? Absolutely.

But that day I learned a lesson that I keep relearning. That day I discovered who I was without my lipstick. With all my flaws, and with all the problems life would throw at me, I've discovered that come what may, I am a child of God. And, as a child of God, I am equipped to do what He has called me to do through Christ who gives me strength (Philippians 4:13).

We all have our lipstick. For me, that was literal on the day of an important lunch appointment. But usually the lipstick is merely a metaphor for anything a woman feels she needs to make her attractive, appealing, interesting, strong, or ready to do what God has called her to do. The fact is, we need nothing more than what God has put inside of us.

Please don't misunderstand me here. I'm not against

makeup. There's a lot to be said for maximizing our looks if you enjoy that, and I do enjoy that. I love large pieces of costume jewelry. I genuinely appreciate it when someone takes the time to put forth effort to improve anything. I enjoy sprucing up an outfit, my living room, and even my office. I'm all in favor of paint and polish and upgrade. But I am against the false sense of security that can come from anything the world offers that tries to replace our value to God. Our worth is in the fact that God loves us and He has called us. It's in the substance that is within us, not in anything else.

LIVING FROM THE HEART

You may remember the television show *I Love Lucy*, which many women my age and younger grew up watching. When my daughter Chloe was about six years old, she had seen the *I Love Lucy* episode in which Lucy and Ethel got stuck in the shower fully clothed as water filled to the top and, of course, disaster followed. But as you can imagine, it looked amazingly fun to a six-year-old, so she and a friend decided to recreate it in our walk-in shower.

Complete with bathing suits and pool toys, they plugged the shower drain with a towel and proceeded to fill it with water. But just as the water was about two feet high, they decided they had experienced enough "fun" and did just what you would expect. They opened the shower door! As gallons of water filled the bathroom floor, I rushed to see what all the commotion was about. Needless to say, it was a huge mess and extremely funny all at the same time.

Our worth
is in the
fact that God
loves us and
He has called
us. It's in the
substance that is
within us, not in
anything else.

As Chloe tried to explain her "Lucy" moment, she made a poignant comment: "Mommy, as we were doing this, my head said yes and my heart said no. How do I learn what's right?" I responded to her sincere question, "Always listen to your heart. If you know Jesus, He will tell you what to do in your heart. And, if you will choose to listen, you will get along much better in life."

Living from the heart is unconventional. The world around us teaches us to live according to the head. Often we think only with our heads or we use our human powers of reason. We think about the obvious, the norms, or the business-as-usual in our heads when our hearts are screaming something entirely different. If we're not careful, when we think with our heads, we'll make the mistake of ignoring what our hearts know to be true and right.

> Living from the heart is unconventional. The world around us teaches us to live according to the head.

With our heads, we try to analyze, but our hearts are designed to simply believe the things of God. While our heads evaluate situations and look for perfection that probably never exists, our hearts may miss hearing God's voice calling us into the right way to go or leading us to the supernatural gifts God has prepared for us. Sometimes hearing with our hearts makes more sense than hearing with our heads ever will.

Perhaps under what our heads notice lie amazing things we never noticed about ourselves or about the people around us. As human beings we have a keen knack for observing the obvious. But what about observing not only the obvious but all that God has for us?

I recently read several articles about the human brain. Science now asserts that each person has three brains, not one, that send what I'll call "thinking signals."[2] Those three places are the head, the heart, and the gut. We can think of these as the mind, the will, and the emotions. All of these are talking to us at once, and all are trying to get us to listen! Pause and think about that.

The Bible talks about the "still small voice" (1 Kings 19:12), that is, the gentle nudging of God's Spirit, His precious voice giving us an impression, a feeling, a knowing. Some call it "gut instinct." It's a gift of emotional sensitivity from God, which He has placed particularly and strategically in us for divine information. We don't have to ask whether God is speaking. The question is, are we listening? And if we are listening, what are we doing with the precious information He communicates to us? The information can be processed in three ways. First and perhaps most dangerous, we can ignore it. Second, we can use it unwisely or wrongly. Or third, we can use it as God intended for our benefit and for His.

I well remember the day God got my attention concerning His desire to let me "feel" His still, small voice deep within my gut. I was driving home from an appointment and had three small children at home with a babysitter who was on a very tight schedule. I didn't want to make her late. However, as I was nearing home, I clearly heard a still, small voice say, *Turn your car around and go buy the outfit you looked at last week.*

I thought, *Okay. That's a good idea, because it is for someone else, and I think it will be a nice blessing for her. I'll just go do that—later!* But again I heard the same voice, same message, this time much stronger. *Turn the car around, and go buy that outfit first. Now.* I thought, *Okay, but what's the big deal? It's just an outfit.* Or so I thought! Without further questions, I turned the car around, went to the store, and bought the outfit. It only took a few minutes. But during those few minutes, there was a horrible accident in exactly the spot I had been headed.

As I pulled my car off the road and heard the sirens wailing, I heard that voice clearly again, only this time it was soft and really sweet, saying, *I wasn't concerned about the outfit, I was concerned about your life.*

I couldn't move. I couldn't drive. I just sat in the car on the side of the road and cried. I cried tears of repentance for thinking I knew better than the One attached to that still, small voice. I thanked my heavenly Father for loving me so much and for allowing me to hear with more than just my natural ears.

Ephesians 3:18–19 says that God's love for us surpasses head knowledge and is so vast and immeasurable that it's hard to comprehend it. But if we ask Him to speak to our hearts and process His words in our spirits, we can really hear and know the heart and will of Father God.

Without our metaphoric lipstick, without all the trappings of this world, we are women of substance and immeasurable worth. We have an essential nature that is at the heart of who we are. It has nothing to do with what goes on in our heads. It's where our true life in God takes place. To become women God can use, we must live from the heart, not the head, regardless of our lipstick. So, game on! Let's do this thing.

To become women God can use, we must live from the heart, not the head, regardless of our lipstick.

2

MARY MAGDALENE, JOANNA, AND SUSANNA: THE GUCCI GIRLS

Three ordinary yet completely different females. A celebration of all that makes us unique and all that binds us together as women.

At first glance, these were just average ladies with everyday lives, likely overseeing the practical matters of running their households. They probably dealt with relational issues, aches and pains, and whatever stresses accompanied life in New Testament times. I'm sure they had to reconcile their hopes and dreams with mundane realities, just as you and I do.

At the same time, these were not just your average, everyday ladies. As I mentioned in the introduction, they are named in Scripture—Mary Magdalene, Joanna, and Susanna—and that is a big deal. They were remarkable women of substance, and their willingness to provide for Jesus out of what they had made them extraordinary.

> Now it came to pass, afterward, that He went through every city and village, preaching and bringing the glad tidings of the kingdom of God. And the twelve were with Him, and certain women who had been healed of evil spirits and infirmities—Mary called Magdalene, out of whom had come seven demons, and Joanna the wife of Chuza, Herod's steward, and Susanna, and many others *who provided for Him from their substance.* (Luke 8:1–3, emphasis mine)

These three short verses—this account of Mary Magdalene, Joanna, and Susanna—can reshape your life and release you into the very best God has for you.

As I said in the introduction, many readers of Luke 8 (myself included and maybe you too) seem so focused on the parable of the sower in this chapter that we may have overlooked the three important women who set the stage and created the atmosphere for this scenario to play out. They, and others, facilitated Jesus' ministry by providing for Him "out of their substance," meaning their resources—whether spiritual or financial.

My father-in-law was convinced that Mary Magdalene, Joanna, and Susanna serve as role models for women today and that today's women can be as significant to what God is doing now as those three were centuries ago. He truly felt that in the next cohesive move toward Jesus' return, women could play a key, strategic role, just as they did in Luke 8.

Jesus was a planner, and He knew the end from the

beginning. Although Jesus had not yet left the earth when the events of Luke 8 unfolded, Oral believed that in this account Jesus seemed to be preparing something integral to His return. The idea of "women of substance," Oral said, would pave the way for women to be, in many ways, in the forefront of establishing the atmosphere for God's great plan for humanity, as Jesus expressed it in prayer to His Father: "Your kingdom come. Your will be done on earth as it is in heaven" (Luke 11:2). Jesus' intention is for us to experience abundant life in Him while living on this earth and then for us to graduate to our eternal life in heaven to live with Him forever.

Mary Magdalene, Joanna, and Susanna found their proper place in God's kingdom. They were valuable to Jesus' ministry while He walked the earth, just as women are valuable to the church today. Those women made provision for Jesus' ministry—that was their seat of authority and their proper position. And women today can do the same.

Too many women feel insignificant or inept when it comes to serving God's kingdom in authority and strength. Every person has a proper position in Christ—his or her own place, a seat of authority Christ has purchased at the cross. Therefore, I'm calling for women today to rise to that strength and authority.

Before you start to think I'm proposing a feminist revolution in the church, let me stress a point I mentioned earlier: this revelation is not to push men out of their rightful place in God's design but is for women to be strong enough and spiritual enough to take their own place. There's room enough in God's kingdom for everyone. In fact, everyone is needed, wanted, valued, and created with a glorious purpose. Mary Magdalene, Joanna, and Susanna fulfilled their purpose as they provided for Jesus out of their substance. That's what they were called to do, and they obeyed. Their story can help you fulfill yours too. Let's consider what happened that day, the day Jesus told the parable of the sower.

MORE THAN MEETS THE EYE

Can you imagine three more completely different women? Talk about diversity! They were three remarkable women, each exhibiting different traits and representing a different walk of life. Based on outward appearances, they should not have been sitting in the same airspace together, let alone working together for the good of the Lord. When Mary Magdalene, Joanna, and Susanna were together, to the natural eye, the room would have appeared to hold a former demon-possessed woman, a quiet lady of means, and the wife of King Herod's CFO (chief financial officer). Joanna's husband was Chuza, a steward in the royal household of Herod Antipas. In today's language, his position would be comparable to that of a CFO, business manager, or property manager. He may have been a political appointee.[1] What in the world were these three doing together? They certainly did not appear to have anything in common socially or economically.

Women often tend to assess others based on external qualities, and that would have been easy to do with Mary Magdalene, Joanna, and Susanna. When we give in to the temptation to carefully or even critically examine only the outward appearance—height, weight, hair, makeup, clothing, jewelry, financial status, and other external aspects—we almost always guarantee that we will never know the greatness that lies within the individual before us. There is a lot we do not know about Mary Magdalene, Joanna, and Susanna, but we do know this one thing: they loved Jesus. And that overcomes every societal barrier, outward appearance, or life experience.

UNITING AROUND JESUS

Imagine the protocol of those New Testament days and picture Mary Magdalene hanging out with the wife of a very powerful man in the Roman government. Mary was from the city of Magdala, which, according to the Talmud, was a place known for prostitution. For this reason, people have assumed for generations that she was a prostitute. Many scholars also believe she was the sinful woman mentioned in Luke 7:36–50, just prior to the account we are considering in Luke 8. While Scripture never says that she was a prostitute, we can safely assume she had a troubled past, perhaps including indiscretions and improprieties, if not prostitution.

Because of Mary's background, she probably could have been arrested for requesting entrance into the person's residence where Jesus was teaching the parable of the sower. And what would the women there be talking about? Certainly not their professional lives! If this account happened today, would these women have the same friends, frequent the same restaurants, drive similar cars, dress alike, or attend the same parties? I don't think so!

Imagine a glimpse into the encounter if it were to happen today. It may not be too far-fetched to think it might go something like this:

"Hi, I'm Mary."

"Oh really? Hi Mary, what do you do?"

"I'm from Magdala, so you know what people think. They think I'm an adulterer. Some even say a hooker."

"Oh really? Where do you work?"

"In the city."

"Oh really? Do you know my husband, the bigwig?"

"Oh, is he a client of mine? No? Maybe? Are you sure?"

"Great hair."

"Thanks. You too. Are those Gucci?"

"Ya."

"Mine are Frederick's, you know, the kind they have in Hollywood."

"Have you had any great sushi? I hear there's a new place in town."

"No. I don't get out much during the day. I work at night. Sleep most of the day. I had these seven demons that used to manifest at will, and I'm not sure, but I think one is manifesting now. Oh no, oops, my bad! That's over now!"

What are the chances of this happening? And yet there was a former demon-possessed adulterer, or as some called her, a prostitute (either way all the name-calling certainly wasn't pleasant), out of whom Jesus cast seven demons, talking with a woman whose family was huge in politics, and Joanna, the "hostess with the mostess," putting this whole shindig together. Great party. Really rockin', girl!

I don't think so.

And yet. And yet! What was Jesus thinking? What could He possibly have had in mind when He became the center of this motley crew, this "girl bash chick time" social gathering?

I believe He told us exactly what He was thinking. And it's not about what we think; it's about what Jesus knew. He was introducing us to the concept of women of substance, women of worth, and making sure He included us all— from the prostitutes to the political set, from the lowest to the highest, to show that any woman from anywhere can become a woman of worth at any time if Jesus becomes the center of her life. He was demonstrating 2 Corinthians 5:17, which teaches us that when we repent before the Lord, old things—old patterns, old behaviors, and even old labels—can go away, and all things can become brand-new.

> Any woman from anywhere can become a woman of worth at any time if Jesus becomes the center of her life.

LET'S THINK ABOUT THIS SPIRITUALLY

Looking at this gathering from a spiritual perspective, we would discern three women of faith who had much in common: purpose, calling, and assignment. By evaluating the hearts and souls of these three women, rather than their outward appearances, we can gain an accurate, godly glimpse of women of substance and worth, women God used to minister to His Son and further His mission on earth.

The woman from the street, Mary Magdalene, the formerly demon-possessed woman, recognized Jesus for who He is. Of all the people to see Him for who He is. Go figure. Mary Magdalene's thought life reflected her renewed state of being, her new life in

Christ, where old things (old behaviors of the flesh) went away and all things became new (2 Corinthians 5:17).

One of the primary keys to living in victory is learning to think spiritual thoughts rather than earthly thoughts. Human reasoning, clouded by envy, pride, jealousy, tradition, or simply wrong judgment, might just fool you. But godly thoughts, obtained by renewing your mind daily with the Word of God, are completely different.

God looks at the heart because it reflects the invisible spiritual realm that we cannot see with our natural eyes but is real, active, and more influential on Earth than some people realize. Sometimes we may deliberately choose not to see the spiritual because acting out in the flesh is so much more exciting to talk about, right? Spiritual thinking, however, is the place where our belief system exists. It's where our filter can receive or reject God's thoughts. So, in the flesh, the scenario of these three women is ridiculous. Naturally speaking, before they met Jesus, these three women would not even think of being in the same room together. But since they had committed their lives to Jesus, they now followed the same Lord. Receiving Jesus' cleansing power by an act of faith qualifies any person to represent Jesus in any setting He so chooses.

The question, therefore, is not, What in the world did these women have in common? Now the question is, What in Christ Jesus did they have in common? When we understand that Jesus brings people of like faith together, we are able to see instantly why these women were in the same room. The common denominator is Jesus Himself, the One who is well able to draw people together in unity, in one accord, for one purpose. As women God can use, we have a common goal to carry out His plan as we live "in Christ Jesus" and reflect His image in the way we live.

MIRROR, MIRROR, ON YOUR WALL

Remember the line from the evil queen in *Snow White*, "Mirror, mirror, on the wall . . . ?" If so, you may also remember that she asked her mirror, "Who's the fairest of them all?" We assume she was hoping the answer would be something like, "You are, of course!"

I think some of us remember that line because we have a mirror on our wall, and it shows us who we are on the outside. It doesn't reveal anything about who we are on the inside. But we tend to give it more power than any shiny piece of glass should ever have.

What's the word for women today, including you and me? Do we just sit back and become like Eve in the book of Genesis? Eve, God's precious creation, the woman with the forbidden fruit who didn't finish her course and fulfill the purpose God had for her. I often wonder how God felt about that. Some may think He was upset, but I think He was sad because He knew all He wanted her to become, and He watched as she chose not to follow the path that would enable her to do so.

Or do we see ourselves as modern-day Bathshebas? She made mistakes. Yet she earned the heart of the king and the respect of the kingdom. No longer just the woman history remembers as the one with whom King David sinned against God, she eventually raised a son to lead the kingdom in such a way that it is at least a possibility that the transformation in her life was so godly that she could be regarded as the Proverbs 31 woman, wife, and mother.

With all the social media pressure to follow an "all about me," gossiping, backstabbing, get-ahead culture, is it possible that we women could lay aside our differences—even vast differences—to do the true will of the Father?

The way I see it, Oral was onto something. He saw it. He knew it. And he was convinced that it was not only possible but that it was God's desire to see His beautiful creation walk a beautiful path. No longer would we walk the way of suffering. Because Jesus already walked that road for us, our destiny is now to walk the pathway of righteousness, which, simply put, means "right relationship" with Father God, His Son Jesus, the Holy Spirit, and ourselves and others in God's kingdom.

WHERE ARE TODAY'S WOMEN OF SUBSTANCE?

We've already answered the question *What did Mary Magdalene, Joanna, and Susanna have in common, as diverse as they were?* But that leads us to ask, *What in the world could Mary Magdalene, Joanna, and Susanna have in common with women today? How are they relevant in our fast-paced, modern, internet, Facebook, Twitter, Instagram world?* The one everyone talked about behind her back, the hostess with the mostess, and the society chick most certainly went through what women go through today.

Nothing has changed except the passing of time. From then until now, there have been mean girls, society girls, sleazy girls, gossip girls, pretty girls, popular girls, and on and on. Nothing changes except their names. They all face the same problems, hurts, failures, successes, and challenges. The question is not, Where are *those* women? We know the answer to that one. The question is, Where are the women of substance, the ones who recognize their worth? If they were important to Jesus when He walked the earth, they are equally important today.

So let's do what Jesus did. Let's break the mold of the way the world—and even some in the church—expect women to be. Let's cut a new path and discover all God has for us as His much-valued, much-needed women of worth in this precious place called life, just as Mary Magdalene, Joanna, and Susanna did.

3

IF IT'S BROKEN, FIX IT. IF IT'S NOT, LEAVE IT ALONE. BUT DO NOT GIVE UP.

It's common to think that to come to the Lord we have to be perfect, but perfection isn't what God is looking for. God looks for excellence but certainly not perfection. As women, though, we often strive for perfection in ourselves, in other people, in things, and in relationships, but the broken and the imperfect are all around us. Thankfully, many situations, relationships, people, things, and aspects of ourselves are in good shape. They may not be perfect, but they are not broken, and they don't need fixing.

I've noticed that many women put themselves under great stress trying to fix what is not broken and trying to avoid fixing what is broken. An important key to a peaceful, powerful life is embracing and enjoying what's going well while also addressing what needs work.

An important
key to a
peaceful,
powerful life
is embracing
and enjoying
what's going
well while also
addressing
what needs
work.

IT LOOKED PERFECT, BUT . . .

It's impossible to overstate how much preparation went into the perfection of the *Titanic* to make it the best of the best to impress the best of the best. It cost $7.5 million to build in 1912, which, if we account for inflation, would be approximately $200 million today,[1] and it took fifteen thousand workers to construct it. It contained:

- a swimming pool
- two libraries
- a Turkish bath
- a gym
- a squash court
- twenty thousand bottles of beer
- fifteen hundred bottles of wine
- eight thousand cigars

The *Titanic* even had its own newspaper on board, reporting on the news, stocks, horse racing, and society gossip of the day. The most expensive first-class ticket on this magnificent vessel cost $4,350, or more than $50,000 today.

The ship had every luxury a wealthy traveler could want. But even with all the planned greatness of the *Titanic*, you know what happened: it sank. Epic perfection became epic failure. The ship appeared to be perfect, but it wasn't.

As I researched the *Titanic,* I was shocked to learn that some sources say that in spite of all the things the ship did have, it didn't have something vital to a successful voyage:

binoculars. Other sources say that binoculars were on board but not accessible to the crew.

With no binoculars available to the crew—along with too few lifeboats, no lifeboat drill, and lifeboats with empty seats—no wonder the *Titanic* episode is called a disaster. Key systems that should have been in place to avoid danger and preserve life simply broke down or were never implemented. For our purposes, we could say that many things about the *Titanic* were "broken." Someone should have fixed them before it was too late.

This teaches us that the "big" things aren't always the most important things. The Turkish bath and fifteen hundred bottles of wine sank with the ship. It's often the little things, like binoculars, that make the most significant differences in our lives. Perhaps if you feel like you can't do all God has called you to do until it's on a grand scale, you'd consider being willing to be faithful over the seemingly little things because you never know when they will become the big things. God's not looking for grandeur; He's looking for a heart that wants to serve Him. Remember, He's the captain of the ship of your life. He doesn't need a perfectly rendered plan to keep you afloat and move you forward. He simply needs your whole heart.

> The "big" things aren't always the most important things.

POTATO-POTAHTO; TOMATO-TOMAHTO

If the account of the *Titanic's* sinking is a story of many intricate details tended to and yet a story of epic failure, the story of ketchup is quite the opposite. Unlike the *Titanic*, no detail was set in stone and no one really agreed on what formula was the best for success. The *Titanic* teaches us that things can appear to be wonderful yet be seriously broken, while ketchup shows us that something can be unbroken, even great, yet people keep tampering with it.

The quest for good ketchup became one experiment after another until someone finally got it right. Unfortunately, the story didn't end there. Once they got it right, they just kept messing with it until they could have destroyed what we know today as "Heinz, the thicker, richer ketchup."

Ketchup comes by way of a lot of experiments and, interestingly, by way of a lot of oceans. While there are many different stories of how ketchup came into being, the stories do include *kecap*, also spelled *ketjap*, as an Indonesian word that somehow morphed into a Chinese word *ke-tsiap*. Originally, ketchup was a form of fish sauce typically made with fermented anchovies dissolved in brine. Imagine that on your french fries today.

In the 1600s, European cooks experimented with ketchup by adding mushrooms, walnuts, oysters, and even lemons, along with anchovies. While salt was always consistent, many recipes included vinegar and sweeteners to the soupy, runny sauce. Around 1812 Dr. James Mease, a physician-horticulturist from Philadelphia, continued to experiment with the formula, and he is the one who added tomatoes to the recipe to move it toward the ketchup we know today.[2]

Finally, by 1872 Henry J. Heinz developed the recipe his company still uses to this day. Interestingly, Heinz used ripe tomatoes, sugar, onions, vinegar, and spices. His goal was to touch all the major taste components—sweet, salty, sour, bitter, and even what we would consider savory.

IF IT'S NOT BROKEN, DON'T
MAKE IT PURPLE

Ketchup as we know it today was not tampered with for many years, and the H. J. Heinz Company became one of America's most successful companies. *However,* one day after more than a century of success, someone decided that Heinz ketchup needed updating. The proverbial "Why mess with success?" suddenly fell by the wayside, and the Heinz company decided to experiment.

While they kept the original ketchup recipe exactly the same, they decided to create pink, blue, teal, orange, and, yes, even *purple* ketchup. And though the basic recipe remained the same, somehow people didn't jump at the opportunity to put pink or teal tomato sauce on their french fries. Fortunately, for all of us ketchup lovers, Heinz went back to the original plan and stayed the course of success, teaching the great lesson that if it isn't broken, stop messing with it.

Some people simply can't leave a good situation alone. In our desire to be used of God, we can fall into that trap. Sometimes the Holy Spirit is leading us to pray, but we want to act instead. So, rather than pray, we do something—and make the situation worse. Sometimes the Holy Spirit wants us to hold our peace and keep our mouths shut, but we just can't bear being silent, so we say something—only to realize the Holy Spirit was right, of course, and we should not have said a word.

To fulfill God's call on our lives, we must pay attention to His timing and His instructions. His instructions could involve addressing situations that need attention, even though they may look wonderful. Otherwise, the ship could sink. And we must be sensitive to God's timing and instructions, learning to keep our hands off and our mouths closed when we don't need to intervene.

LITTLE FLORENCE, BIG DREAMS

Sometimes in our attempts to fix something that needs to be fixed or to discipline ourselves to leave alone what's not broken, our biggest mistake is that we quit too soon. To illustrate this thought, consider a woman named Florence.

Florence Chadwick, born in 1918, was an American woman who simply liked to swim. The more Florence would swim, the more she wanted to swim, until one day she decided to swim the English Channel—both ways. All she had going for herself was her swimming ability and her inner drive to accomplish something that no woman had ever accomplished before. No one invested millions of dollars or sophisticated equipment in her venture. No one conducted experiment after experiment to make her better. In 1950 thirty-one-year-old Florence crossed the English Channel in thirteen hours and twenty-three minutes, traveling from France to England, and then a year later she swam from England to France.[3] Ultimately, she was able to swim the English Channel four times.

An interesting twist to this amazing story took place in 1952. Florence was from the California coast, and she had a deep desire to swim the twenty-one-mile journey between Catalina Island and the California coastline. To keep her encouraged, as well as to ensure her safety from sharks, small boats accompanied her.

Fifteen hours into this amazing journey, thick fog blanketed the water. Not only did fog roll in, but discouragement rolled in as well. Florence signaled one of the surrounding boats, the one carrying her mother, to pull her out of the water and into the boat. Assuming the worst, people began to wonder if she was sick. Did she simply run out of energy? Was she just not strong enough? Did the shark-infested waters take a toll on her emotions, causing her to be overcome with fear? Her reason for stopping wasn't as glamorous as they supposed.

Sadly, Florence quit because she couldn't see the finish line. The fog had clouded her judgment, and she quit too soon. She simply lost sight of her goal. As she was being pulled into the boat, she was told that she was only a short distance from reaching her goal. Some sources say she was half a mile, while others say she was about a mile. Either way, she was almost there.

Imagine a woman capable of swimming the English Channel four times allowing something as simple as fog to create such doubt in her abilities so close to reaching her goal.[4]

How often we need to be reminded of Galatians 6:9, which says we must not become weary in doing good, for we shall reap rewards in due season if we don't quit.

DON'T PARK BESIDE YOUR FAILURE

Regardless of how or why Florence quit, she did not reach her goal. But an important thing to know about Florence's story is that she did not park beside her failure. Florence did not look at Catalina as defeat. She simply saw it as an opportunity to try again. And try she did!

Florence set out once again to swim the Catalina Channel only two months later. As if to mock her amazing determination, the fog rolled in once again. This time, however, Florence Chadwick would not be shaken. She refused to quit. She later told of the mental image of the shoreline that kept her going throughout the entire swim.[5] She did not think of the fog; she didn't focus on the past failures or even the past successes. The only thing Florence focused on was the goal set before her. It was the quintessential eyes on the prize necessary to succeed.

This time the outcome was totally different. Not only did she reach Catalina, but to prove her amazing determination to rewrite her own story, Florence went on to swim the Catalina Channel on two more occasions.

NOW, WHAT ABOUT YOUR STORY?

Often we may feel that our previous defeats define us, but I want to remind you of Florence. Not only did she refuse to let the previous defeat define her, but she used it to push her closer and faster to the finish line. We need to remember what Paul wrote, "One thing I do, forgetting those things which are behind and reaching forward to those things which are ahead, I press toward the goal for the prize of the upward call of God in Christ Jesus" (Philippians 3:13–14). When we simply trust God and reach out in faith believing, He is "able to do exceedingly abundantly above all that we ask or think" by his power working within us (Ephesians 3:20).

Things of the past and even the present may try to discourage us. But the way to achieve the prize, which is in Christ Jesus, can be as simple as reaching forward with our faith. An amazing thing about the Christian life is that when we do our part, God is faithful to do His. Our part is the easy part: we believe God and take Him at His Word, and He watches over His Word to perform it (Jeremiah 1:12).

WHAT CAN WE LEARN?

From the sinking of the *Titanic*, we learn that perfection is not always the answer and rarely even possible. From Henry J. Heinz, we learn that there is no need to mess with God's formula set forth in His Word. Once God establishes what He wants for our lives, all we have to do is stick with the plan. It's not our job to keep changing and adjusting the plan (unless God says to do so) or to think we know better than His plan. Our job is simply to follow the plan and see the road of God's success.

From Florence Chadwick, well, that's an easy one! Fog does not have to define us. From Florence's story, we can see that losing sight of the goal is temporary, but victory lasts forever if we are willing to take every experience in life, good or not so good, and put it to productive use. If we can learn that pain and disappointment can somehow actually become powerful, there is no telling what results we will experience if we keep our focus where it needs to be—on God and His Word. There is no limit to the goals we will accomplish and all we can do to shine for the kingdom of God when we allow God to do His part in our hearts and lives.

BATHSHEBA: THE GOSSIPED GIRL

You've heard of her, right? Bathsheba, the woman who took a bath on her roof and found herself the object of a king's desire, so much so that he would send for her, sleep with her, get her pregnant, scheme to make her his own, and order her husband to certain death on the front lines of a battlefield so that he could take her for his wife. We can read this sad account in 2 Samuel 11.

That's a whole lot of wrong for a woman to go through to get to the right place. Now, you might be asking, "Bathsheba—right place? When was she ever in the right place?"

How did she get to be a wife of the king of Israel? The Bible doesn't say she signed on for all that. We don't know if she intended for David to catch a glimpse of her bathing as he walked the roof of his palace. We don't know if, when he sent for her, she hurried excitedly to his chambers or went with trepidation, knowing she simply was not allowed to say no to the king. We don't know if she wanted to have an affair with King David or if she knew about his scheme to kill her husband and take her for his own wife. But history, like human nature, often assumes too much. And because human nature leans toward whispers and bends toward gossip, people are prone to assume the worst, even in the face of the best.

For Bathsheba, I wonder if the rumors began like this: "She must have been looking for trouble. She must have seduced David because she was bathing where she knew it was easy for him to see her. She must have been a willing adulterer. She probably started the affair—after all, she slept with him. She must have been looking for royal status because maybe David wanted to make her queen. And she must have been a partner in crime because David had her husband murdered so she would be free to marry the king."

Bathsheba must have been bad, right? Well, the Bible doesn't say that. The Bible indicates that the problem started with David, not with Bathsheba (2 Samuel 12:1–13). Scripture tells us it was spring, the time of year when kings go to battle—only David was at home in his bed (2 Samuel 11:1–2). So, probably, was everyone else because it was evening. Maybe David couldn't rest. Maybe he was tossing and turning, thinking of all the battles the other kings were waging, and thinking he should be with his men, fighting those battles. In any case, he was restless, got up, and went for a walk on the roof. And the rest is biblical history.

"Yes," some might whisper, "but she must have been trying to seduce him, bathing where he could see her." See how that works? See how much some people assume and how ready some are to see the worst? We are told just enough to wonder and let our imagination run wild, right? Now Bathsheba is the topic of gossip. Many of us can relate to the pain of being unfairly gossiped about and to all that can go terribly wrong when this happens.

THE PROVERBS 31 WOMAN UNVEILED

One of the strangest Bible lessons I learned was something Oral talked about regarding Bathsheba and the Proverbs 31 woman—this absolutely perfect person whom so many women strive to become but can never actually accomplish. She was not Mary Poppins, who was "practically perfect in every way," but the Proverbs 31 woman was pretty amazing. She was so amazing that almost an entire chapter in the Bible describes her. She's not named or identified, but her wonderfulness and accomplishments are on full display. A woman of true worth! Oh, to be that brilliant, amazing, cool, warm, hardworking, perfect woman, the ultimate woman, the Bible's "it girl."

One day my scholarly father-in-law told me I needed to study Proverbs 31 and get back with him about it. There was much more to this "perfect woman" that I had overlooked. So I studied, and oh, what I found. The more I studied not *what* she was but *who* she was, the more shocked I was at what I discovered. Who, if anyone, was this glorious chapter and glorious woman patterned after? Answer: no one really knows for sure. Speculation: she could have been Bathsheba.

That's right. Jewish legend suggests that Lemuel and

Solomon were the same person. Therefore, in her older years, Bathsheba, Solomon's mother, could have been the Proverbs 31 woman. Some say this woman whom the writer of Proverbs calls "virtuous" (v. 10) and "blessed" (v. 28)—this portrait of a godly woman, this one we've been told is our role model and believed was so perfect that she set the standard for all females to follow—was Bathsheba.

Let's consider this theory. If it's true—and that's a big *if*—then Bathsheba—the mistress, the betrayer, the one King David lusted after and for whom he murdered—would have made a long, courageous journey after she married the king. She would have been through a lot to become the woman God designed her to be. Just what if the mother of King Solomon, the wise mother who advised David to pass the kingdom to Solomon over all other siblings, was the one who started out "that woman" and ended up another woman—a woman of God, a woman of courage and worth, the woman regarded as the gold standard for Christian women today?

What? No way, I thought. I was not reading these commentaries correctly. I mean, how many Bathshebas could there be in the Bible? The only one I knew of was *that* Bathsheba, the sleaze, King David's adulteress. So it had to be some other Bathsheba, right? If not, this concept ruined every single Bathsheba Bible study I'd ever heard and reduced the Proverbs 31 woman to a real person, a human being, a *flawed* female. This couldn't be right, and I felt as though all my sermons on Proverbs 31 needed a delete button.

Could the Proverbs 31 woman *really* be Bathsheba? Or is all this just crazy talk? Well, that's a good question. And it's one about which scholars still disagree. But there are those who think Bathsheba is the woman behind Proverbs 31, and some who even think she possibly cowrote it with her son. How is that possible?

Let's take a look at the reasons some people think Bathsheba, giving her son Solomon advice about finding an excellent wife, is the Proverbs 31 woman. The question being answered in Proverbs 31 is basically, Who qualifies as a godly woman, a godly wife? Who better to give advice than Bathsheba—a woman who knew exactly what not to do and who not to be? She had plenty of experience, after all. And if she really did undergo a transformation from a woman of sin to a woman of God, she would know exactly what to tell him to look for. Who better to teach a son than a mother who started out with a huge mess in her life and ended up better than she could have imagined?

We know Bathsheba began her walk of fame as the woman for whom David risked his kingdom and displeased God. While some people view Bathsheba as a victim, others think of her as the worst of the worst, an adulteress and a seductress. But while her failures have been broadcast on the front page of many believers' hearts and minds, how many of us also recognize her as the one who birthed a future king? Bathsheba raised their son Solomon to carry on the godly kingdom that David (in his repentant state) built to glorify and honor God.

As David grew older and the godliness of the kingdom was in jeopardy, it was Bathsheba who told David which ungodly son was going behind David's back to turn the kingdom away from God. Bathsheba's daring persistence and boldness provided David with information to preserve the kingdom as David built it and kept it righteous for God. It was also Bathsheba who birthed and raised King Solomon, the beloved son, who finished the temple as God intended and carried on the kingdom as God instructed.

Even today Christians worldwide highly regard Solomon and teach about his riches and wisdom. He is credited with the writings found in the other chapters of Proverbs and was king at the time Proverbs was written. Therefore, he could be the king referred to in these chapters. It is also possible that Lemuel was King Solomon's nickname. Whether scholars will ever agree on this aspect of Jewish lore remains to be seen. The mystery may never be solved. And perhaps that is as God intended.

But regardless of what certain scholars believe, the part I find baffling is why some think Bathsheba could never progress into anything or anyone beyond the woman who seduced David. According to the Bible, David sinned, repented, and was a man after God's own heart. David was a great man, a great leader, and a great king. But he *did* sin and he repented as well. Most Christians focus more on his greatness than on his sin. So isn't it possible that through all these obvious signs, Bathsheba actually changed and grew into a godly woman, helping her godly husband raise a godly son to secure a kingdom's godly future?

David repented, and because of that we see his greatness and his excellent finish in God. Why can't we see that same progression—into sin, out of sin, into repentance, and into greatness—for Bathsheba, especially when everything else the Bible records about her points to such?

Why do some people leave Bathsheba in her sin? Why not allow her to grow in God? Why couldn't she be the Proverbs 31 woman, Solomon's mother, and even a mother who helped her son author a chapter on what to seek in a godly woman? Who better to pen a chapter on success than a person well acquainted with failure? Who better to pen a chapter on the goodness of God than someone who has lived in both sin and virtue and has seen exactly what the goodness of God can do?

Who better to pen a chapter on success than a person well acquainted with failure?

Who among us can't relate to Bathsheba in some way as the one who sinned or the gossiped-about girl or the one not just stuck in her past but seemingly cemented into it? Whether or not we have sinned exactly as Bathsheba did, we all have made mistakes or sinned, and we know that it can make us miserable.

THE HUMAN FACTOR

Romans 3:23 says we all have sinned and fallen short of the glory of God. I call this "the human factor." God knew when He created us that as humans we would make mistakes. God knew from the beginning of time that the only sinless, perfect One would be Jesus. God sent Jesus so we could have the opportunity to repent of our "human factor."

Although I could share many personal stories of God meeting my "human factor" needs, no story of knowing the power of Christ's love is as important to me as the day my son died.

At age eighteen, I was told I would never have children. After surgeries, difficult medical reports, and two miscarriages, this seemed to be my path. But I finally carried a baby to full term and delivered a perfectly healthy baby boy. To say I was overjoyed is an understatement. I believed my suffering was finally over, and I knew I had been blessed by God to have a child.

Within thirty-six hours after his birth, our son was lying dead in our arms because of a quickly developed breathing problem. Devastated and facing the giants, especially the never-satisfied media giants, I was in no shape for what lay ahead. The media mongers worked overtime declaring Oral Roberts to be the loser of the civilized universe, so vile that he couldn't muster up enough *whatever* to save his own grandson, his own namesake, my son.

In less than a day and a half, I birthed a child, buried my child, and then had to tell the world what happened. This was tormenting to say the least. On the way out of the memorial service, I was confronted by a curious man who said he had a question for me. Numb, I stood there and said, "Okay."

He asked, "What do you think of your Jesus now that your son is dead?"

I was speechless. I wanted to get angry, to yell back at him, *Are you kidding? Now you ask me that? Right here, right now?*

How I came up with an answer, I don't know. It could only have come from my spirit, because my heart, soul, head, and physical body were exhausted.

I turned to him and said, "I have never felt closer to God and closer to my Savior than in this horrible time of need."

How could I truly know the Waymaker until I'd totally lost my way—the pain in which I found myself that day? That was my test, at the most inopportune time in my life. But as I looked back, I discovered it was the perfect time. The real test of my faith and what I thought about God did not come as I tiptoed through the tulip fields of life. It was in the hellhole of despair that I found my real faith, my real trust in God. It was the worst possible way I could imagine discovering who He is and who I am, but I discovered it for sure that day. The human factor was at its worst, but God's love was as strong as ever.

> It was in the hellhole of despair that I found my real faith, my real trust in God.

SEEING CLEARLY

While my situation was completely different from Bathsheba's, my mirror-mirror moment was the same. The mirror-mirror moment is when, no matter how you got there, you find yourself looking life squarely in the face and discover that the only one staring right back at you is *you*. No bloodsuckers, no media hounds, no gossip grubbers, no parenting critics, no dysfunctional families, no boss, no mean Christians who act like the devil. No one but you.

At that moment, you can discover how you see you. Not the tainted opinions of others, but how you see yourself. Then you can open the door wide to see how God sees you—just as you are from His point of view. If there is one thing I've learned after many years of being a Christian, it's this: *God sees me from an entirely different vantage point than others do. He sees me completely differently even than I see myself.*

When we look in the mirror, our appearance is exactly what we see. When we put a camera on a subject and take a picture, what comes out? Exactly what we took the picture of. Why?

Because what we focus on is what develops. What we focus on will manifest. What we dwell on is what we just might become.

> What we dwell on is what we just might become.

Whatever people think in their hearts, they become (Proverbs 23:7). So often we let the opinions of other people cause the Word of God to have no effect on our lives (Mark 7:13). When the labels, whether they are man-made or self-inflicted, become all we see and all we focus on, is it any wonder we live up to them? But what if we could get past what we see and instead, like God, see what we *can* become, what He has created us to be?

At some point, the mirror must no longer be our enemy but become our inspiration to see ourselves through the eyes of God, transformed by His Son, Jesus Christ.

At some point, Bathsheba had to stop seeing herself as "that woman" and see herself as a woman forgiven and changed by the power of God. At some point, she must have seen herself not as the product of her past, but as the future person God desired her to become—a godly wife and mother, and perhaps even the framework of the Proverbs 31 woman now admired by Christians everywhere.

Did she have regrets? I'm sure. Hope? Of course. A great future? Absolutely! So here is the question: How do you see yourself? Do you see the old you, like the old Bathsheba, always in a mess or at least remembered for some mess? Gossiped about, insulted, and the topic of every potluck dinner or ladies' luncheon?

Or can you choose to change the focus on the lens of life and see yourself with a hope and a future? Can you see yourself as God sees you, as God has always seen you?

My prayer is that the next time you look into the mirror, you can see heaven's precious reflection of you. You will see yourself beginning to become the "new Bathsheba," the awesome Bathsheba, the Proverbs 31 Bathsheba, the woman of worth and value God sees when He looks at you.

5

IF LIFE WERE A
ONE-ACT PLAY . . .

Many times I've looked at life as if it were a one-act play, a drama unfolding before my eyes. Now, let's clarify something here: drama is not trauma. They are two totally different things that need to be dealt with differently. Drama is drama, and according to *Lexico*, it is defined as "an exciting, emotional, or unexpected series of events or set of circumstances."[1] Well, well. This definition sure describes my life. Does it sound familiar to you? While my life has had its twists and turns, I certainly can say it has been exciting—and emotional and unexpected! Therefore, it can be described as drama—thus the idea of a one-act play.

If my life really were a one-act play, however, I would love for the script to be written by someone like David. We've talked about him some in the previous chapter as Bathsheba's husband. He was a man acquainted with drama. But he was also a man familiar with restoration. He experienced, caused, and put up with all kinds of drama throughout his life, but the Bible says that "David *recovered all*" (1 Samuel 30:19, emphasis mine). Although this verse refers to a specific incident, I do think the idea of recovering all is biblical. It's certainly happened in my life, and I could never have orchestrated it for myself. God did it. So I like the idea of recovering all. I *really* like it, and I believe it is possible with God (Matthew 19:26).

Let's look at a little history of King David's life. While it's true that David was king, he didn't start out that way. He was not born into royalty. Actually, there's a good bit of information and speculation about King David's humble, if not questionable, beginnings and unusual past. Miriam Feinberg Vamosh, who holds an MA in archaeology and heritage from Leicester University and has written many articles and books on life in Bible times, believes that King David's mother was a household servant of Jesse, David's father.[2]

David referred to his mother in Psalm 69:8: "I have become a stranger to my brothers, and an alien to my mother's children." Then, according to Got Questions, legend is that his mother was named Nitzevet, meaning "standing woman," or a working woman in that time. Like Vamosh, the researchers at Got Questions see the validity in the possibility that David's beginning was different from that of his brothers, and perhaps that sheds a flicker of light on why his brothers were so harsh toward David and why his father ignored him as a possible candidate for king (1 Samuel 16:11).[3]

Why is this digging into David's history even important anyway? Speculation can come from many sources, including gossip. It can come from lack of information about the past or about our families, and it can stem from rejection. I can't even begin to tell you how many things I've had to deal with in my life based on gossip, mere speculation, the unknown, or even on questions about family. As a result, I learned one thing: the most important opinion of me, the only one that really matters, is what God thinks of me.

Perhaps you are currently in a place that I have been in many times. Perhaps some of the questions about your life—your beginning, your middle, or even right up to this point—have created a vacuum of speculation or gossip or rejection or something similar, or perhaps like me, some of it is the great unknown and you have little knowledge of certain things in your life. I want to encourage you to believe that, as in David's case, the one opinion that really matters is God's opinion, and move forward. Allow God to do something in you, as He did in David's life.

What do we really know about David? We know for certain that he began as a shepherd boy and then became a soldier. As a soldier, he went through battles. He needed that experience to be qualified to reign as king. In David's story, and perhaps in some of our personal stories, battles are the situations that cause us to find our strengths and weaknesses and to gain the experience we need to make progress on our journeys.

WHAT WAS DAVID THINKING?

Drama and recovery are the themes of David's story—the man after God's own heart. About the time David moved ahead of a situation, along came something else to deal with. But a verse at the end of a tragic episode of loss in 1 Samuel 30 summarizes how David overcame and how you can too: "David recovered all" (v. 19). Earlier in chapter 30, we read that David's family and other men's families had been overtaken and kidnapped. But David and his army pursued the kidnappers and retrieved all their families and possessions (vv. 1–19).

Like David, about the time I find momentum to move forward and step out after a situation has tried to stop me, Satan pursues me with something crazy, such as sickness or surgery, or the death of a loved one, or people acting like the devil coming against my family or against the ministry—and the drama starts all over again. About the time I dedicate myself to moving forward, Satan shows up, making me wish I had never started that particular journey.

Ephesians 6:12 says, "We do not wrestle against flesh and blood," but our battle is "against principalities, against powers, against the rulers of the darkness of this age, against spiritual hosts of wickedness in the heavenly places." That's a spiritual way of saying that the battle is not with people and that people are not the cause of our problems even if they appear to be. Behind most of the attacks we face is the spiritual force of the devil himself, who comes against us to steal, kill, and destroy. But this scripture also says that Jesus came to earth to give us life more abundantly: "The thief does not come except to steal, and to kill, and to destroy. I have come that they may have life, and that they may have it more abundantly" (John 10:10).

Throughout my lifetime—spent studying the Word of God as much as possible and sitting under the instruction of Oral Roberts—in the middle of battles, I still find it easy to forget that Jesus said He came to bring life to His people. That includes all believers, like you and me! It's easy for us to focus so much on the devil's role—to steal, kill, and destroy—that we forget the part that declares that Jesus came to give us abundant life. It's easy to talk about the problem and focus on the problem, so that all we see is the problem. We can become fixated on life's drama and forget that God's plan for us is total recovery.

THE TORNADOES OF LIFE

Tornadoes often take place in Oklahoma, where I live. I have heard the sirens and felt the stillness of the calm before the storm. Even in the middle of the hottest dampness and humidity, there is a certain chill in the air. Then it hits. As the twister comes roaring out of the air, your entire soul can feel the rumble of what's happening, like the rumble of an oncoming train. Once the initial storm passes, the first thing many people do is go outside and assess the damage.

What happens in the aftermath of a tornado is just like what happens with the storms of life. Once the initial storm is over, the drama of the aftereffect is still there. Many times, in the midst of the drama, it's difficult even to think of recovery. But this is where the women mentioned in this book can help you discover your true worth.

WHAT'S ON THE OTHER SIDE OF YOUR MIRACLE?

I want to share with you one of the most important questions anyone ever asked me so that you will have the opportunity to think about it the same way I did. Right smack in the middle of dealing with the death of my son, my father-in-law, Oral, requested that we have "one of those" talks. I was not in the mood for one of those talks or any other conversation.

Simply to appease him, I agreed to listen. Meaning no disrespect (I always loved my time with Oral), I just wasn't emotionally ready to talk to anyone about what I was going through. Thinking this conversation would be a long, drawn-out theological Oral Roberts discussion, I was prepared just to smile and tune out everything he said. But instead of a long talk, he simply asked, "What miracle is on the other side of this mountain for you? What miracle is just waiting for you to discover it?"

That sentence bypassed my ears and went straight into my heart. I had a lot to think about. For the first time, I genuinely realized that I did not have to put up with the attacks of the devil. I began to focus on what was on the other side of my believing.

It was like what David asked when he decided to take on Goliath: "Is there not a cause?" (1 Samuel 17:29). Was there a genuine reason to go forward in battle and face the giant? In my case, metaphorically speaking, I was looking into the eyes of the giant of miscarriages and death when my father-in-law asked me whether I was willing to go forward in my battle to have children and face the giant. Was there not a cause? What really was waiting on the other side of that important question needing an important answer?

> Waiting for me on the other side of the pain I was going through was recovery.

Something went off in my spirit that made me draw on every statement of faith I had ever known. I now know that the reality of the answer to Oral's insightful question was simple. Waiting for me on the other side of the pain I was going through was recovery. Waiting for me on the other side of miscarriages, surgeries, and the death of my son were the births of my beautiful daughters, Jordan, Olivia, and Chloe. Waiting for me on the other side of surgery and cancer was the opportunity for me to tell you my story of total recovery.

"NO, DEVIL: IT IS WRITTEN . . ."

When I finally saw who my enemy was and what he was trying to do to me, I had to decide to activate the authority I had according to God's Word. By focusing on the situation or the people who had somehow hurt me, I was always living in the pain of what had happened or what they had done. When I decided to go after the devil through prayer and faith in God, however, I now could say what Jesus said when the devil tried to get Him off course. As Satan threw biblical half-truths at Jesus, Jesus simply replied: "It is written . . ." (Matthew 4:4, 7, 10).

As Satan hurled things against me, I could have tried to reason things out in my head, which resulted in no concrete solutions to fix things. But when I switched my words to Jesus' words and declared, "Devil, it is written . . . ," I went from fear to faith and from nothing to something. And that something was hope. I went from hopelessness to genuine hope in Jesus. Joshua 24:15 says, "Choose for yourselves this day whom you will serve. . . . But as for me and my house, we will serve the LORD." I had to choose whom I would serve. I had to tell the devil no to his plan for my life, and when I did, things began to change. I really believe you can do that too.

I've been told that the word *cry* used throughout the Bible has two totally different meanings. *Cry* can mean to express feelings of "Oh, boo-hoo, poor me. I'm so defeated." However, it also means "battle cry." I made a decision to stop the "boo-hoo, poor me, the devil is attacking me" kind of cry. Since then I have been in battle-cry mode. That means I can resist the devil and demand him to flee as I submit to God (James 4:7).

I encourage you to do what I did and declare by faith, "Devil, I call you defeated, and I declare my victory in Jesus' name. Amen."

Deuteronomy 30:19 teaches that we can choose blessing and choose life. I have made the decision to choose life, and you can too. Jesus said that not only can we have life, but we can have life more abundantly—over and above, more than is necessary, exceeding, superior, more excellent, and extraordinary (John 10:10; Strong's G4053). That's what Jesus declared, and if it works for me, it can work for you!

WHEN PAIN FINDS PURPOSE, IT BECOMES POWERFUL

Pain is powerful. There's no doubt in my mind that the devastating pain I went through years ago has now found a purpose through this book, and that purpose is to cause you to believe that you, too, can become a woman God can use powerfully.

With that established comes the easy part. In case you're rolling your eyes, wondering how recovery could be the easy part, I want to tell you a story. It's found in 2 Kings 6:8–23, and it recounts the prophet Elisha's experience with the dramas of life—with no hope of recovery in sight.

Elisha and his servant were in a city, surrounded by the army of Israel's enemy Syria. During a battle against Israel, the Syrian king wanted to capture Elisha because Elisha's prophetic gift had enabled him to tell the king of Israel what the Syrians' next move would be (v. 9). Understandably, this ability to anticipate the Syrians' attacks frustrated the Syrian king, so he decided to capture Elisha (vv. 12–13). Elisha's servant woke up one morning and realized he and Elisha were surrounded by the Syrian army, along with its horses and chariots (v. 15).

To the natural eye, Elisha seemed doomed. His servant thought they would both be killed, but Elisha prayed to the Lord, "Open his eyes that he may see" (v. 17). Immediately the Lord revealed to the young man the angelic hosts surrounding them. Then God blinded the entire Syrian army, and Elisha led them into the city of Samaria where they were given food and sent back to their own country. The amazing thing is that during this time, Syria never attacked Israel again (vv. 18–23).

The most important part of this story is that Elisha and his servant understood the simplicity of believing God and trusting that He knows best. As long as they submitted to God, everything went according to God's plan. When the people involved decided that God's plan of success was far better than any plan of failure the devil had, God's plan took over. When we are willing to trust God with the drama in our lives, we can open the door for God to operate His plan of redemption called total recovery.

According to Lexico, the word *recover* means "return to a normal state of health, mind, or strength" and "find or regain possession of (something stolen or lost)."[4] *Strong's* interlinear online defines *recovery* as "rescued, saved, delivered (from enemies, troubles, or death); to deliver from sin and guilt."[5]

When God sets in motion the process to recover all, He is talking about restoration. Restoration is the scriptural recompense of reward found in Hebrews 10:35: "Cast not away therefore your confidence, which hath great recompense of reward" (KJV). *Strong's* interlinear online defines *recompense of reward* as "requital."[6] Collins defines *requital* as "something given or done in return; repayment, reward, retaliation, or compensation."[7] Merriam-Webster defines *requital* as "something given in return, compensation or retaliation."[8]

God wants our confidence to be our fearlessness, our boldness, and our assurance in God. He promised the recompense of reward. The "great reward" of our confidence and faith means He will compensate us for or return to us what is rightfully ours.

Hebrews 10:36 tells us we have "need of endurance," which means we should not lose patience. Patience can be defined as loyalty to faith and sustaining perseverance.[9] Then Hebrews 10:38 says, "The just shall live by faith." There is no changing the fact that the Bible says we are to demonstrate our belief in God. When we declare and demonstrate our belief system in God, we can experience Him as the Rewarder.

God says that He will become our recompense of reward when we simply trust Him by asking Him to forgive us of any wrongdoing and declare the reestablishing of our belief system in Him. Therefore, in God's due season (Galatians 6:9), drama can shift into God's responsibility concerning recovery.

O MY SOUL

Bless the LORD, O my soul;
And all that is within me, bless His
    holy name!
Bless the LORD, O my soul,
And forget not all His benefits:
Who forgives all your iniquities,
Who heals all your diseases,
Who redeems your life from destruction,
Who crowns you with lovingkindness and
    tender mercies,
Who satisfies your mouth with good things,
So that your youth is renewed like the eagle's.
                    —PSALM 103:1–5

One key to recovery is in the realm of the soul—the mind, the will, and the emotions. The recovery may manifest in the physical realm or the external activities of your life, but it can start on the inside. When our minds (thoughts) align with God's Word, we use our will to make decisions that agree with His Word, and then godly feelings follow.

We are to renew our minds daily with the Word of God. The Bible instructs us concerning our thoughts: "For the weapons of our warfare are not carnal but mighty in God for pulling down strongholds, casting down arguments and every high thing that exalts itself against the knowledge of God, *bringing every thought into captivity to the obedience of Christ*" (2 Corinthians 10:4–5, emphasis mine). The reason we are to take every thought captive is that when we do, we are moved out of the plan and purpose of the enemy and springboarded into the amazing miracles God desires for us.

Jesus came to earth to "destroy the works of the devil" (1 John 3:8). This means that any attack of the devil—past, present, or future—can be replaced with a miraculous plan of God. Jesus can direct your path, and you can live in the reality of Jeremiah 29:11: "'I know the plans I have for you,' declares the LORD, 'plans to prosper you and not to harm you, plans to give you hope and a future'" (NIV). That is an amazing promise. Right now, as you reach out to God in an act of your faith, let me encourage you to believe and declare these words:

- God has a plan for me, and that plan is to prosper me so that I have a successful journey on the road of life.
- God wants no harm to come to me.
- God has plans to give me a hope and a future.
- God has amazing miracles for me.
- As it applies to my life, I release shame, blame, negative thinking, and negative words, and I replace them with the words of God.
- My mind and my mouth are not created for a mess. My mind and my mouth declare God's miracles.

As you speak these words of declaration and act on the Word of God, allow Him to start making you more and more a beautiful woman of tremendous worth.

6

Esther: More Than
Just a Pretty Face

Best known as *Queen* Esther, Esther was not even her birth name. Her parents, about whom little is known, gave her the name Hadassah. The woman we know in the Bible as Esther was a Hebrew orphan (a Jew) raised as a daughter by a relative, Mordecai, in Persia (Esther 2:15).

Vashti was the reigning queen of Persia. Her husband, King Ahasuerus, considered her beautiful, so beautiful that he enjoyed showing her off. One fateful evening, while Ahasuerus had a group of friends and advisers visiting the royal palace for a seven-day feast, he called Vashti to come to the throne room, wearing her royal crown, so that he could display her beauty. But the queen refused to come (Esther 1:5, 10–12). Ahasuerus was astonished and enraged and even perhaps embarrassed by her behavior. His advisers immediately counseled him to get rid of her, worried that if she was allowed to refuse the commands of the king, other women would also "despise their husbands" and bring chaos to the kingdom (v. 17). With this strange turn of events, Vashti's behavior became Esther's passport to the palace.

THE KING MUST HAVE A WIFE

Vashti's rebellion resulted in her banishment from the throne. The king called for a new wife and launched a search to find the most beautiful young women in all the Persian lands (Esther 1:19; 2:1–4). Esther was one of the women chosen as a potential candidate, and Mordecai warned her not to let anyone know she was a Jew (Esther 2:8, 10). Each day, Mordecai walked by the court of the women's quarters at the palace, hoping to find out that Esther was doing well (v. 11).

The preparation process for candidates hoping to be the king's new wife was intense, with a full twelve months of beautification treatments. A different woman was selected each day for the king to see (vv. 12–14). According to verses 15–17,

> Now when the turn came for Esther the daughter of Abihail the uncle of Mordecai, who had taken her as his daughter, to go in to the king, she requested nothing but what Hegai the king's eunuch, the custodian of the women, advised. And Esther obtained favor in the sight of all who saw her. So Esther was taken to King Ahasuerus, into his royal palace, in the tenth month, which is the month of Tebeth, in the seventh year of his reign. The king loved Esther more than

all the other women, and she obtained grace and favor in his sight . . . so he set the royal crown upon her head and made her queen instead of Vashti.

One day Mordecai learned of a plot against Ahasuerus and revealed the plot to Esther. She told the king about it and let him know that Mordecai had alerted her to it, and the king's life was saved (Esther 2:21–23). Esther rose to a new level of prominence after this and went on about her duties for four years.

Notice that Esther continued doing what she had always done for *four years.* Think about that. We live in an instant society. We have instant oatmeal, instant coffee, instant internet, Instagram, and so on. Yet in Galatians 6:9 the Bible encourages us to be sensitive to God's timing, saying, "Let us not grow weary while doing good, for *in due season* we shall reap if we do not lose heart" (emphasis mine). God's timing isn't always instant, but we are wise not to get ahead of God, His plan, and His perfect timing.

It's easy to allow discouragement and weariness to set the course for our success if we don't get instant answers or see immediate results. But by allowing God's perfect timing to play out, we can begin to see His plan unfold in the best way He chooses. Letting God and His judgment determine that timing removes from us any pressure to become driven by what could be an improper schedule. Proverbs 19:21 says, "There are many plans in a man's heart, nevertheless the LORD's counsel—that will stand." By allowing God's plans and His purposes to prevail, we allow His success rate to prevail as well. So why throw our humanity into the mix? God is God, and His wisdom is on a completely different level than ours. As Isaiah 55:9 says, God's ways are higher than our ways, and His thoughts are higher than our thoughts.

THE STORY BEHIND THE STORY

History records the immense persecution of the Jewish race. To fully understand the story of Esther's courage, it's important to consider the culture and the men involved in her world. Shortly after Esther was crowned queen, Haman, a descendant of wicked King Agag of the Amalekites, was promoted to grand vizier and became the number-two official in Persia. Mordecai, however, honored God and was a Benjamite from the lineage of King Saul. In the past, Haman's ancestors had battled against Mordecai's ancestors in a long-running feud, which could explain Haman's particular hatred for Mordecai and his people (Exodus 17:8–16; Judges 3:13; 1 Samuel 15:1–35; 30:1–5). And when Haman found out that Mordecai was a Jew, he began to scheme against all Jews.

Against this backdrop, Mordecai advised Esther to keep her Judaism a secret, fearing that she could be killed if her heritage were to become known. To make matters worse, Mordecai refused to bow to Haman. Knowing he could not deny God and bow to wickedness, Mordecai was now targeted for his beliefs.

Furious about Mordecai's refusal to pay homage to him, Haman approached the king with a bribe and news of a people who observed godly laws and did not keep the king's laws (Esther 3:1–9). Ahasuerus told Haman to keep his money but allowed him to do as he pleased with these unnamed people (v. 10). Acting in the king's name, Haman issued the command to kill all the Jews living within the borders of Persia (v. 13). When Mordecai heard of the edict, knowing what it meant to God's people and even to Esther herself, as she was a Jew, he immediately sent word of the proclamation to Queen Esther, along with a request that she intervene (4:1–9).

DEFEATING THE SPIRIT OF FEAR

Fear is one of the harsh realities of life. When Mordecai beseeched Esther to approach King Ahasuerus on behalf of the Jewish people, she had to defeat fear or allow fear to defeat her. This was no small request. Anyone who went before the king without being summoned was subject to execution.

Concerned, Esther sent a message back to Mordecai that she had not been summoned to visit the king for more than thirty days (Esther 4:10–12). In the back of her mind must have been the fact that her husband had a huge issue with disrespect. No doubt she remembered what happened when Queen Vashti did not honor him.

Mordecai reasoned with Esther that even a resident of the palace could not escape the decree of the king and reminded her of her Jewish roots that put her in just as much danger as Mordecai and every other Jew (Esther 4:13). It was then that Mordecai asked Esther one of the most famous questions in the Word of God: "Who knows whether you have come to the kingdom for such a time as this?" (v. 14).

I don't believe for a moment that God brings trouble to us. But He does give us the ability to learn from it and even shine in every situation in which we find ourselves.

AN UNDERUSED WEAPON THAT STILL WORKS TODAY

Esther agreed to approach King Ahasuerus, but with a powerful condition—the underused spiritual weapon of prayer and fasting.

Mordecai had to agree to focus the faith of the Jewish population through three days of prayer and fasting before Esther would do his bidding. After that had happened, she was willing to risk an audience with her husband, saying, "And so I will go to the king, which is against the law; and if I perish, I perish!" (Esther 4:16).

THE EXTENDED SCEPTER

Calling on her faith and summoning all the courage she could muster, Esther entered the throne room and waited for the king to acknowledge her. What happened next is remarkable:

> So it was, when the king saw Queen Esther standing in the court, that she found favor in his sight, and the king held out to Esther the golden scepter that was in his hand. Then Esther went near and touched the top of the scepter. And the king said to her, "What do you wish, Queen Esther? What is your request? It shall be given to you—up to half the kingdom!" So Esther answered, "If it pleases the king, let the king and Haman come today to the banquet that I have prepared for him." Then the king said, "Bring Haman quickly, that he may do as Esther has said." So the king and Haman went to the banquet that Esther had prepared. (Esther 5:2–5)

God gives
us the ability
to learn from
trouble and
even shine in
every situation
in which we
find ourselves.

Not only did Esther have favor, but Ahasuerus declared that she could have anything she wanted—*up to half the kingdom of Persia*. She took a tremendous risk and was rewarded with unprecedented favor.

ESTHER POSITIONED HER ENEMY TO FALL

Esther then did something unusual and strategic. She invited the king and Haman to another banquet, one to be held the following day, at which time she would make her petition on behalf of the Jewish people (Esther 5:7–8).

Haman left the first banquet on a high note. When he caught a glimpse of Mordecai standing in the king's gate, he thought about Mordecai's refusal to honor him, and he was "filled with indignation against Mordecai" (v. 9). After boasting to his wife and friends about his privileged position, he followed their suggestion to build a seventy-five-foot-tall gallows on which to hang Mordecai. His plan was to hang his adversary in the morning as soon as he could secure the king's permission (vv. 10–14).

A SLEEPLESS NIGHT THAT
TURNED OUT WELL

Unable to sleep that night, Ahasuerus had "the book of the records of the chronicles," a record of his reign, read to him (Esther 6:1). In the reading was a record of Mordecai's warning about the plot against the king. Further investigation revealed that Mordecai had not been rewarded for his efforts (vv. 2–3).

Immediately, Ahasuerus began devising a plan to honor Mordecai. The more he thought about his plan, the better he seemed to like it. Meanwhile, Haman had come to the palace to suggest that the king hang Mordecai (vv. 4–5). When Ahasuerus encountered Haman, the king, thinking of Mordecai, posed the question, "What should be done for the man whom the king delights to honor?" (v. 6).

ARROGANCE POSITIONS PEOPLE FOR COLLAPSE

When the king asked Haman how he would honor a faithful and trusted lifesaver, Haman arrogantly assumed King Ahasuerus wanted to honor him. He replied,

> For the man whom the king delights to honor, let a royal robe be brought which the king has worn, and a horse on which the king has ridden, which has a royal crest placed on its head. Then let this robe and horse be delivered to the hand of one of the king's most noble princes, that he may array the man whom the king delights to honor. Then parade him on horseback through the city sqaure, and proclaim before him: "Thus shall it be done to the man whom the king delights to honor!" (Esther 6:7–9)

Imagine Haman's shock when he first realized that the king was not honoring him but Mordecai—the man Haman planned to hang! "Then the king said to Haman, 'Hurry, take the robe and the horse, as you have suggested, and do so for Mordecai the Jew who sits within the king's gate! Leave nothing undone of all that you have spoken" (v. 10).

THINGS CAN ALWAYS GET WORSE
FOR THE ENEMIES OF GOD

As bad as things were for Haman, they were about to get worse.

The king chose Haman to lead the horse and announce the greatness of Mordecai to the people of the Persian capital: "So Haman took the robe and the horse, arrayed Mordecai and led him on horseback through the city square, and proclaimed before him, 'Thus shall it be done to the man whom the king delights to honor!'" (Esther 6:11).

Instead of living in disgrace, Mordecai returned to his place of government service. According to Esther 6:12, "Afterward Mordecai went back to the king's gate. But Haman hurried to his house, mourning and with his head covered." Can you imagine Haman's thoughts in that moment? He knew the rules. He was about to receive a death sentence for deceiving the king. Things were not looking good for Haman!

NO COMFORT FOR EVILDOERS

Not wanting to seem like accessories to this imploding disaster, Haman's family and friends offered him no consolation: "When Haman told his wife Zeresh and all his friends everything that had happened to him, his wise men and his wife Zeresh said to him, 'If Mordecai, before whom you have begun to fall, is of

Jewish descent, you will not prevail against him but will surely fall before him'" (Esther 6:13).

The Holy Spirit was quick to confirm their negative assessment: "While they were still talking with him, the king's eunuchs came, and hastened to bring Haman to the banquet which Esther had prepared" (v. 14).

Responding to Queen Esther's earlier request for the king and Haman to join her for a second banquet, the two men went. Queen Esther had a story to tell and a petition to submit.

The king set her up perfectly, asking what she wanted and reminding her that he would give her up to half the kingdom (Esther 7:2). Her story was plain and the petition to the king was a pointed one. Queen Esther boldly said,

> "If I have found favor in your sight, O king, and if it pleases the king, let my life be given me at my petition, and my people at my request. For we have been sold, my people and I, to be destroyed, to be killed, and to be annihilated. Had we been sold as male and female slaves, I would have held my tongue, although the enemy could never compensate for the king's loss." (vv. 3–4)

The king seemed genuinely surprised by Queen Esther's request and asked her, "Who is he, and where is he, who would dare presume in his heart to do such a thing?" (v. 5). Then Esther had her moment, her chance to identify the enemy of God's people, saying, "The adversary and enemy is this wicked Haman!" (v. 6). In that instant, Haman, who had been so angry and indignant toward Mordecai, so crafty and unfair toward the Jewish people, and so arrogant was "terrified before the king and queen" (v. 6). Then the king arose in his wrath from the banquet of wine and went into the palace garden (v. 7).

AN ACT OF PANIC SEALED HAMAN'S FATE

Seeing his own demise looming before him, Haman began to beg for his life. He threw himself across the couch where Esther was sitting. Ahasuerus returned to find Haman far too close to the queen. He accused Haman of attempted rape and asked what should be done to him. Someone in the royal court suggested Haman be hanged on the gallows he had built for Mordecai. Haman's fate was sealed, and he was hanged on the gallows in front of his own house (Esther 7:7–10).

ESTHER STILL HAD WORK TO DO

The king gave Esther all Haman's possessions. Esther then revealed that she was related to Mordecai and conveyed Haman's properties to him. Ahasuerus promoted Mordecai to prime minister of the government of Persia. Only King Ahasuerus had more power than Mordecai.

Esther may have started her life as an orphan, but she didn't finish it that way. As Queen Esther, she lived her life as a courageous, selfless, godly woman whom God used mightily. An entire nation had her to thank for their lives. It's important for us today to realize that the king making Esther his queen went far beyond the king's choosing. This royal position was God's choosing to uniquely position Esther and establish the king's trust in her so her voice could be heard at a critical time in the future. Once King Ahasuerus had opened his palace to her, she was able to be used by God in time of great need for the Jewish people, her people. Her position of authority was a door opener. You see, Esther was not beautiful so she could become queen; Esther was beautiful to save a nation.

DELILAH: QUEEN ESTHER'S TWIN?

Delilah. Queen Esther's twin sister. Well, sort of—except for the whole Samson, destroy-a-nation incident.

You may be asking, "Which Delilah are we talking about here? Because if it's the one who destroyed Samson, how could she possibly be related to the beautiful Queen Esther?"

The answer is simple. Both were anointed women with tremendous qualities. They both were gifted communicators, obviously. But how can they be compared in terms of the essence of who they were, let alone be regarded as twins? One definition of *twin* is this: "something containing or consisting of two matching or corresponding parts."[1] Another definition is "one of two persons closely related to or resembling each other."[2]

And if you look at these two amazing women, you will see remarkable similarities. In fact, in many ways they were almost identical. Both were physically beautiful. Both were able to capture the attention of very important and powerful men. Both had a clear assignment and were committed to carrying out that assignment as fully as possible. Both women were faced with an all-or-nothing situation. Both women understood who God was. Both women understood the potential of their own power and influence.

But there's a big *however:* while Esther took a huge risk to get the attention of the powerful King Ahasuerus, she did it for the saving of a nation. Delilah did it for the destruction of a nation. Delilah was in it for herself, while Esther was in it for God.

STUPOR, NOT STUPID, BUT BEWARE

As I was thinking about this, I began to research an unusual state of animal behavior called *katanixis.* We can see how the word *catatonic* could come from this, and it does. It's like being in a stupor. I learned a lot about this from a television documentary on sharks and the state of a shark when it is put into what is called shark catatonic immobility, a natural state of paralysis that animals can enter—at least the animals that were tested. The animal is put into a state of immobility either for its own benefit or for the safety of someone or something in harm's way. In the case of a shark, it will actually flip upside down.

On the program, a scientist demonstrated this power or authority, if you will, over a shark. I was amazed. And out of the blue, two thoughts came to me. First, Delilah's power to mesmerize Samson was similar to the way the scientist mesmerized a shark. It seemed so unnatural yet so easy.

My second thought was that the predator was so willing to surrender to the prey. How is it possible to get something as powerful as a shark to submit to an outside source of authority so easily? It seems like it should be harder. There should be more resistance. But being mesmerized is powerful.

While Esther was trying to get Ahasuerus's attention for important matters, such as the love of God and country, Delilah was trying to captivate Samson (kind of like the scientist mesmerized the shark) through lustful ways for the purpose of personal gain. Big difference.

Delilah used her powers of self-advancement to destroy Samson and facilitate the downfall of God's nation. Esther risked her life to get the king's attention in order to save the Jewish people.

Delilah was filled with deception and lies. Esther was filled with hope and the truth of God. Esther had everything to lose. Delilah had everything to gain. Therefore, the stakes were completely different. For Esther it was all or nothing; life or death. For Delilah it was all for Delilah's life and death to God's plan.

It's amazing to me that back in 1950, just over seventy years ago, my father-in-law, Oral Roberts, preached one of his most classic messages about Samson and Delilah: "The Battle of Champions." All these years later, the story is the same. The only difference is that occasionally we have different names, dates, and places. History repeats itself over and over and over.

And it came to pass, when she pestered him daily with her words and pressed him, so that his soul was vexed to death, that he told her all his heart. . . . When Delilah saw that he had told her all his heart, she sent and called for the lords of the Philistines . . . and called for a man and had him shave off the seven locks of his head. . . . And she said, "The Philistines are upon you, Samson!" So he awoke from his sleep, and said, "I will go out as before, at other times, and shake myself free!" But he did not know that the LORD had departed from him. Then the Philistines took him and put out his eyes, and brought him down to Gaza. They bound him with bronze fetters, and he became a grinder in the prison. (Judges 16:16–21)

Many know this story as a tale of lust, romance, and intrigue—a woman using her charm to take down a man. But the story of Samson and Delilah is much more than that. Samson was a mighty champion of God whose birth had been announced by the angel of the Lord (Judges 13:2–3). He had been given a sign from God and instructed not to cut his hair (v. 5), which was God's gift to him as the source of his strength. Samson was a Nazirite, and the Nazirite vow meant that he would never touch strong drink or eat anything unclean. He made a vow to be pure and clean and holy before God. He would dedicate his life entirely and completely to God and to His service and to the delivering of God's people.

Samson had extraordinary strength, supernatural power. When the Spirit of the Lord came upon him, he had remarkable, unexplainable strength, which was a sign of his faith in the God he served.

In Samson's day, the Philistines had taken over the nation of Israel. Devastation covered the land at that time and people had barely enough food to eat. God gave Samson great strength and the ability to secure the liberation of the people of Israel.

Samson's remarkable strength enabled him to come against the Philistine army and defeat them. Time and time again, Samson demonstrated his great power from God for the purpose of delighting the nation of Israel and angering the Philistines, who became determined to take down Samson. Because of Samson's strength, you would think it would take an army to defeat him, or at least another strong man. Who would have thought his demise would come at the hand of a beautiful woman named Delilah?

In the Bible, Delilah's first noteworthy quality is her beauty. After that, she becomes associated with all sorts of negative motives, words, and actions. This saddens me, because lovely women throughout history and even today are named Delilah, and they have made this melodious name synonymous with many wonderful qualities. I believe there was a God-opposing spirit that operated through the biblical Delilah and has operated through others for generations and to this day. It is a manipulating spirit by which they control people through seductive behavior designed to distract them and keep them from fulfilling God's purposes for their lives.

> A Delilah is anything or anyone that takes a person away from God.

We could talk about Delilah's beauty and her ability to bring down Samson. We could talk about her ability to confuse his mind and ultimately destroy his spirit. But a Delilah can come in many forms. It can be male or female, or it can be in something other than a person. *A Delilah is anything or anyone that takes a person away from God.* It can come in the form of money, power, lust, hate, unforgiveness, bitterness, disobedience, or some other ungodly element. It's not Delilah the person, but the manipulation and actions involved in trying to move someone out of obedience into disobedience.

POLLUTION CONTROL

Second Corinthians 6:17 says not to touch anything unclean. *Unclean* is very simple. It's anything that pollutes you—your body, your calling, your walk with God, any area of your life.

Samson's family understood this and tried desperately to get him to listen and return to God. But he didn't listen. How often do we ignore good counsel, especially when that counsel comes from someone close to us? Sometimes, in order to recognize wisdom and good advice, we need to hear from an outsider. Sometimes only God Himself can get through to us. The bottom line is not who is talking. The bottom line is, are we listening?

I once heard a story that in the days of the Old West, a stagecoach company was looking for men who could drive stagecoaches through the rugged Rocky Mountains. Many coaches had been lost on the steep and dangerous mountain roads. Many of the applicants were bragging about their ability to drive right up to the edge of a cliff and not crash. But one young man just sat there listening to the others boasting about their driving abilities.

Suddenly he stood and said, "I want to withdraw my application."

The man hiring asked, "Why?"

The young man replied, "If this is the way you have to be to get the job, it's not for me. I'm the kind of man who stays as far away from the edge as possible."

The young man was given the job. The man hiring told him he was just the person they were looking for. "You see, in this business," he said, "it's not about how close you can push it to the edge. It's about how far away you can stay from the edge. That's what will keep you and our cargo safe."

Samson seems to have known exactly how far away from the edge to stay. He made a vow to do that. But instead of doing what he knew best, Samson went as close to the edge as possible until there was no turning back, and he eventually fell over the edge. Many people think they know how far they can go and not go over the edge, but Samson knew that he had to stay completely away from the edge in order to do what God called him to do. And yet once he was committed to the edge, the edge became so easy, so irresistible.

It's interesting that neither Samson nor Delilah trusted each other. There's a red flag right there. To get the secret out of Samson, Delilah had to ask over and over and over again (Judges 16:6, 10, 13, 15–16). That's the interesting thing about sin. Sometimes it's not automatic. Sometimes it starts out as something of deep and total commitment to God, but Satan manages to chip away little by little, until eventually he wears a person down.

It's amazing to me that a man so full of passion for God could lose his vision, lose his eyes, lose his passion, and eventually lose his closeness to God. In fact, his backsliding started out small. He didn't go from all to nothing at his first temptation. He slid little by little until the sin became a gray area and everything suddenly looked the same to him. Right and wrong no longer had a dividing line. The kingdom of God and the kingdom of the Philistines all looked the same to Samson.

What's even more interesting is that he made an excuse for himself, believing that revealing his secret would be acceptable if Delilah really loved him. He knew in his heart that once he told her, there was no going back. Yet somehow he managed to convince himself that it would all be okay.

Notice that this is exactly how Satan works. He messes with our minds and plays with our thoughts. Judges 16:16 says that Samson's "soul was vexed to death." The enemy will do that. The mind is a component of the soul, which is made up of the mind, the will, and the emotions. After a while under Satan's influence, our thoughts take on lives of their own, and then we find that we are not careful with our words. As we read Judges 16, we see that Samson's destruction began with Delilah's words. Delilah's words got inside of Samson's head. As long as they were only in his head, he could deal with them. But once he allowed those words to get deep inside his heart, they began to take over his soul.

Once Samson's thoughts were controlled by Delilah's words, his spirit man began to be controlled by Delilah's spirit. As he kept his mind on Delilah, everything else took a back seat. I'm amazed that she created such all-consuming thoughts in his mind, but maybe that's why Romans 12:2 says that we are to renew our minds with the Word of God.

Delilah can come in the form of anything that creates an all-consuming thought life in a person. Judges 16:20 says that Samson didn't even know the Lord had left him. One of the greatest tragedies in life happens when we stray so far from God that we don't even realize that we have left Him and moved out of His will. The line can get so blurred between right and wrong, good and evil, our calling and something other than our calling. Those blurred lines can become blurred vision, and blurred vision can become blurred passion, and blurred passion can become disastrous.

For Samson, the thought of Delilah was all-consuming. An all-consuming thought can be something simple. It may be negative, such as bitterness, anger, hate, or jealousy. It may also be benign, such as youthful appearance or career accomplishments. The label we put on it is not important. What is important is what it does to you, where it takes you, or what it takes you away from.

While Samson never even realized how far he had gone away from God, Delilah was slowly, carefully calculating each step. From baby steps to big steps, to giant leaps, she meticulously seduced Samson into walking away from God. Finally, she was in his heart and in his head so much that his holy secret became her unholy ticket to fame and fortune. Before he could come to his senses, the woman for whom he gave up everything was busy revealing the secret of his strength to those waiting to give him the haircut of a lifetime.

Second Samuel 1:27 says that someone once thought of as mighty can fall. And Samson certainly was mighty. The Spirit was on him so strongly that he could shake a building. He had God's power. He heard God's voice. Yet he lost something that valuable over a woman. His downfall probably could have been something else, and so could ours—whatever could pull us away from doing God's will. The instigator of Samson's downfall could have been anyone or anything Samson allowed to turn his head! Sadly, for Samson the result was disastrous. Moreover, Delilah didn't even care. It's as though he was in a prison in his mind, and that eventually led him to a Philistine prison.

To top it off, Satan, along with Delilah, made sure that Samson was a public spectacle. He was embarrassed in every possible way. However, his hair began to grow again. God gave Samson a second chance, and the champion was reborn. While the Philistines were trying to show off their conquest, Samson was paraded in the temple of Dagon, a false god worshiped in Philistine culture (Judges 16:23–24). Standing between the two middle pillars of the temple, Samson once again felt the Spirit of God come upon him, and he was able to push apart the pillars, collapsing the temple and destroying about three thousand Philistines (vv. 27–30).

Like Samson, no matter how far we've gone, we can ask for the Spirit of the Lord to return to us. I truly believe that at that point, God will return to us when we yield to His Spirit. If we repent and turn our hearts back to God, we can experience a miraculous rebirth in our minds, wills, and emotions. Samson missed it. He let a mere human being take God's place in his heart. I don't think for a second that we can't love a person with "all of our heart." I realize this is a human saying, but there's nothing wrong with loving a person to the greatest extent of human love, as long as he or she never takes us away from the love, worship, praise, and adoration intended for God and God alone.

God offers hope, healing, and the miracle of a second chance for every woman He loves.

If we repent and turn our hearts back to God, we can experience a miraculous rebirth in our minds, wills, and emotions.

8

DON'T PUT A COMMA WHERE GOD PUT A PERIOD

Isaiah 43:18–19, perhaps more than any other passage, helped me heal after the death of our son, Richard Oral. While I was never prepared for the sheer power of the emotions that would strike what seemed a killer blow to what was left of my soul, I found myself not only at a horrific loss but also in a total emotional mess—a mess in private, a mess in public, and a mess on television.

I had no idea where the rushes of uncontrollable emotions came from and, therefore, not a clue how to manage them. And then—along came Isaiah 43:18–19. I call it the accountability scripture. It left me with no choice but to read it and obey it. After all, it was in the Bible:

Do not remember the former things,

Nor consider the things of old.

Behold, I will do a new thing,

Now it shall spring forth;

Shall you not know it? I will even make a road in
the wilderness

And rivers in the desert.

Forget about what's happened;

don't keep going over old history.

Be alert, be present. I'm about to do something brand-new.

It's bursting out! Don't you see it?

There it is! I'm making a road through the desert,

rivers in the badlands. (THE MESSAGE)

What excuse could I possibly come up with to discount or disregard these verses and simply stay the way I was? I wanted to move forward, but that meant more pain to me. I was conflicted. I was actually afraid. Feelings of fear complicated and compounded the feelings of loss. It was the proverbial "one step forward, two steps back." I didn't know what to do; I simply knew that I couldn't stay where I was. I had to do something, and I genuinely felt desperate. But a part of me was so filled with fear that I felt clueless and, therefore, powerless.

As a side note, during this time I regularly received testimonies from women for whom I had prayed. These were women who had been unable to have babies, and after prayer, God miraculously healed them. Not only did they have healthy babies, but some women even named their babies Lindsay. On one hand, I was overjoyed for them. On the other hand, I was having miscarriages and my baby had died. My head, my heart, and my faith could not explain this. It was as though nothing in my mind could reach a logical conclusion to explain what I was going through.

I realize that women from every walk of life and in every generation in every stage of life go through things that are bigger than they are. If you are living, then the effects of life will *always be there.* And if the effects of life are inescapable, then what? Continue living the way you are living? Oh, please, no! So then what? For me, the answer—the way forward—lay in Isaiah 43:18–19 and a simple rule of English grammar.

As I read this passage, I noticed that it was a command. In fact, it was written to have an understood "you" in the sentence. Literally, this scripture *insists* that you *remember not the former things; that you forget about what's happened.* Since I was the reader of this passage, the "you" meant me! I couldn't act like it wasn't in the Bible.

It was staring me in the face, so *I* had a decision to make. Not Richard, not Oral, not another living soul could do this. It was up to me to believe this scripture or not. In the wake of overwhelming loss and grief, a moment of truth arrived for me. Was the Bible true for *me* or not?

I had to decide what I believed. The goodness of God was either real or it was not, and I had to land on one side or the other. The moment reminded me of Joshua's directive to the Israelites when he said, "Choose for yourselves this day whom you will serve." He gave them the option of serving the gods of their ancestors or the gods of the land where they currently lived. Then he made this powerful declaration on his own behalf: "But as for me and my house, we will serve the LORD" (Joshua 24:15). I felt like one of the women of ancient Israel, face-to-face with the choice of a lifetime: Would I trust God? Would I believe His Word? Or would I trust and believe something or someone else?

At that moment of reckoning for me, Isaiah 43:18–19 seemed to jump right off the page. I saw it. I knew it. God knew it too.

I SAW IT. I SAW HOPE.

While *nothing* had changed concerning my situation, *everything* had changed in me. I had the opportunity to change the situation from my own perspective, when I saw that there was hope for me, when I saw that the Bible meant what it said, when I saw that I could live beyond the hell that I had been living in and move forward with a new thing, and that God would be right there with me every step of the way. I saw one thing and one thing only: hope.

> Absolutely positively nothing had changed. But hope had changed me.

Nothing had changed since I was eighteen years old. Nothing had changed concerning children. Nothing had changed concerning the criticism and the frustration and the public appearance and everything else I was going through. Absolutely positively nothing had changed. But hope had changed me.

I found myself living the reality of Hebrews 11:1. Faith became "the substance of things hoped for, the evidence of things [I had] not seen." As a result, I became new. By faith my situation became brand-new. Everything became brand-new in spite of the fact that nothing had changed technically and physically. But I knew that when I had changed on the inside, everything would change on the outside. With no evidence but the evidence of my faith, I knew that I knew that I knew that I had hope.

After I began to reread and act on Isaiah 43:18–19, a succession of things happened that began to build a foundation and a framework for healing. I felt impressed to give baby showers as often as I possibly could. I made each shower an over-the-top celebration. More times than I can recall, I slipped away from the party and cried in the bathroom until there were no more tears. But I was determined more than ever to follow my father-in-law's instruction and sow a seed out of my need. It wasn't easy. I was sowing in famine. But in spite of the pain, I knew I was sowing into my own healing.

I began to notice there were several directions I could go, depending on how I handled it. I could go forward. I could go backward, or I could stay in the same spot, spinning my wheels with no hope for the future. When I say "no hope for the future," I don't mean coming to terms with never having children. I mean that during that season, I couldn't put one foot in front of the other or put together a positive sentence.

I was hardly existing. Each day I went backward instead of forward emotionally. And that had to change. When I saw hope through Isaiah 43:18–19, I finally felt I could begin to move ahead. Even though my steps were only baby steps, I sensed I was moving. I remembered the story in Acts 28:1–6, when Paul tried to do the right thing by helping people. The more things he did right, the more things went wrong.

SHAKE IT OFF AND FEEL NO EFFECTS

No matter what Paul did, he was persecuted. If that wasn't bad enough, he even had a snake come after him. Many of us probably feel as if we've had people act like snakes coming after us. But Paul had an actual snake attack him (Acts 28:3).

While Paul was shipwrecked on the island of Malta, he gathered sticks to build a fire to keep his entire group warm. He was doing something kind for others when he could have just been taking care of himself. But instead, as he was taking care of others, a snake fastened itself onto his hand. Rather than biting and retreating, it seem to be mocking Paul by pumping in more venom and hanging on just to make the situation worse. The people stared at him, waiting to see how quickly he would die (Acts 28:4).

Paul did not whine, gripe, or complain. He did not talk about the snake, nor did he talk about the venom. The Bible says he shook it off and suffered no harm (Acts 28:5). As people were waiting for him to crumble and die, he miraculously continued to live.

Paul simply shook off the snake. That's a word for us today. When you feel that the devil—or people who behave like the devil—have come against you on every side, you can absorb the venom or you can shake it off.

I've had the opportunity to face those two options, and I have to remind myself to shake off the "snake." In the middle of hurt or devastation, I need to choose to shake it off, just as Paul did.

Philippians 3:14 says, "I press toward the goal for the prize of the upward call of God in Christ Jesus." Isaiah 43:18–19 says not to remember former things because God is doing a new thing and making a way in the wilderness. Both of these scriptures urge us to press forward and not to retreat. To me this is vital instruction for times of pain and difficulty.

When we combine these two passages, they become a powerful road map on the highway to recovery. We can choose to shake off every opportunity for failure. Isaiah 53:1 asks, "Who has believed our report?" We have the opportunity to believe doom and gloom and devastation. Or we can choose to believe the Word of God and make a new road map for our lives.

I think of Hosea 4:6, which says that God's people are "destroyed for lack of knowledge," and of how the devil throws so much against us. Merriam-Webster identifies *pulverize* as a synonym for *destroy*.[1] *Pulverize*, according to vocabulary.com, comes from a Latin word meaning "dust" or "to break down to dust."[2] That description makes me think about why Jesus went to the cross for your healing and mine in every area of our lives. "The reason the Son of God appeared was to destroy the devil's work" (1 John 3:8 NIV). He sacrificed Himself so that we would not be pulverized to dust or destroyed in life, but we must apply knowledge of the Word of God for it to work on our behalf.

> God's mercies are new every morning.

It's time we take God at His Word and turn the tables on the devil. Lamentations 3:23 says God's mercies are "new every morning." I want to encourage you: no matter what you're going through, no matter what you've been through, and no matter what you may be facing in the future, God's mercies are new every morning. I want to repeat these powerful words: *God's mercies are new every morning.* When the devil starts telling you how everything is going wrong and nothing will be resolved, just remember that God's mercies are new every morning.

THE REARVIEW MIRROR OF LIFE

The fact that God's mercies are new every morning means you don't have to live in the past or put up with the past. The past is in the past. Think about it in terms of the rearview mirror of your car. If you're going forward, you'll never reach your destination by looking in the rearview mirror. So, on the journey down the road of life, I encourage you to rip off the rearview mirror of the past (metaphorically) and do as Philippians 3:14 says: "press toward the goal for the prize of the upward call of God in Christ Jesus." In other words, go forward!

Don't put a comma where God put a period. Let go of the things He wants you to let go of in order to move forward. Put behind you the things that need to be in the past. Then let it go, as Isaiah 43:18–19 says:

> Forget about what's happened;
>> don't keep going over old history.
> Be alert, be present. I'm about to do something
>> brand-new.
> It's bursting out! Don't you see it?
> There it is! I'm making a road through the desert,
>> rivers in the badlands. (THE MESSAGE)

"Don't you see it?" means to me that if we are not looking for and expecting a miracle, we could overlook it or even miss it altogether.

Press forward, go forward. Go ahead and make the devil sorry he ever messed with you. Begin to acknowledge the new, powerful you, the woman of worth—the you who will never go back, for "behold, all things have become new" (2 Corinthians 5:17). Tell yourself, "Hello. Nice to meet you, New Me." Embrace the new you and go forward. Period.

9

DEBORAH: A WOMAN OF AUTHORITY AND INFLUENCE

Deborah's name means "honeybee," and it is more than fitting for her. As her name implies, she could have been as sweet and nourishing as honey but still possess the ability to "sting" the enemies of God when necessary. As a civil servant, she was a judge in Israel, but as God's servant, she was a prophetess. Her example and magnificent leadership provide one of Scripture's first validations of women in leadership, women of power—chosen on purpose and not because a man wasn't available—whom God used mightily.

FIND YOUR PLACE

We all have a place, our own place, which God Himself has destined as our spot and in which He desires for us to walk properly. Our goal is to be properly placed, not too far ahead or behind other people, but exactly where God has ordained our destiny. I have known countless women who have felt a strong call of God on their lives, yet struggled to embrace it for various reasons.

Maybe they were afraid of the changes that would be necessary in their lives if they did what God asked them to do. Perhaps their self-esteem would not allow them to move toward all God wanted for them. Perhaps their culture or tradition holds that women "cannot" function in certain ways. Maybe other people discouraged them or even bullied them. Yes, bullies exist in the church. They can be male or female, young or old. They are the ones who try to keep people out of their God-ordained place because they are jealous, because they feel threatened, because they don't want to lose power or influence, or for other reasons.

Regardless of the factors that seek to keep us out of the places God has for us, we can do all we need to do to understand His call on our lives and to walk in it with all our hearts. This, I think, is what Deborah did. A female judge was uncommon, perhaps unheard of, in her day, so we can only imagine what people said to her or about her as she embraced God's plan not only for her, but for all of Israel.

If a true believer, a person claiming to be a part of God's family, were to study Deborah's life, he or she would have to see that God Himself entrusted such power and authority to her and was very satisfied with the outcome of that decision. Now, if God hasn't placed a person in a seat of authority, male or female, young or old, then it's not a godly fit. But when God does place a person, any person, in authority, the fit is right.

If God has placed you in a particular place for a particular job, a particular seat of authority, then are you in it? And if not, why not? Check your seat. It's not about finding *a* great seat of authority; it's about finding *your* seat of authority, your place in God's plan and in His kingdom. If it's your seat, it's a great seat and a great fit.

I'm reminded of what happens in the game of baseball when someone from the outfield bleacher seats steals a seat behind home plate. It's not their seat. It's reserved for someone else! Taking someone else's seat of authority in life is much worse than that, and just because a person can do it, that doesn't mean he or she *should* do it. Just because you can buy a business, steal an idea, or take over a ministry that God hasn't given you and doesn't intend for you, doesn't mean you should. For me it's simple: ask God. Just pray. His decisions are amazing.

The difference between a good deal and a godly deal lies in what's left when all is said and done. With a good deal, one side wins, but a trail of rubble may be left behind. With a godly deal, everybody wins and it takes place without the rubble. I'm all for a good deal but not for a rip-off—a ripping off of the covering, the authority, the seat belonging to another person just because it's vulnerable. People may attempt to justify that kind of behavior, thinking that God left the seat open just for them, but they should first examine their hearts and their motives for taking it. And most of all, they should consider what kind of rubble will be left behind.

I do believe God watches everyone and judges the heart. He's looking to see who is the taker and who stands to profit—the rubble maker or the peacemaker. Who brings peace instead of strife to everyone in the storm? Who carries the peace of God to all involved? We are called to be peacemakers (Romans 12:18) not rubble makers. While opportunity presents itself, God watches the hearts of the opportunists and judges accordingly. How do we handle storms? Who do we hurt? Who do we help? Are the opportunists helping others or merely helping themselves?

God is watching, and if we maintain pure hearts, He will ultimately arrange the proper seating. Then it's up to us to take the seat He has given us. Proverbs 18:16 says your gift will make room for you. Don't worry about what seems to be a mixed-up front-row seating of the chair stealers. God will make things right. His Word says, "Let us not grow weary while doing good, for in due season we shall reap if we do not lose heart" (Galatians 6:9).

> God always balances the scales of justice.

God always balances the scales of justice. Hold on, because in the end, it's God's opinion that places you in your seat of authority. Don't hurry, don't worry, don't grow weary. Choose peace.

Allow God to be the master of ceremonies in your life. His seating chart is always perfect! Think about Deborah. She could have gone to *Christian Gossip* magazine and reported that she defeated the enemy without General Barak's leadership and made him look like a fool (you'll read more about him later in this chapter). But instead, she talked to him, even confronted him, for the overall good of the battle, and got the job done for God. Perhaps we can take a lesson from the godly graciousness of Deborah. She ruled powerfully but graciously and was clearly the leader of Israel during her lifetime.

GOD OFTEN DOES SOMETHING DIFFERENT DURING TOUGH TIMES

Deborah lived during difficult days. The people of Israel had fallen away from God. This was not only a time of backsliding but a time when the nation embraced sin as a way of life. Wars and fighting commonly occurred as God's people forsook His protection over and over. His hand of protection did not move or even waiver in the slightest. But the children of Israel chose to remove themselves from His protective covering and left themselves open to the enemy's attack.

It was during this season of darkness that God chose to do something different. God promoted Deborah to serve as prophet and judge of Israel. Think about that—a judge with the ability to prophesy and a prophet with the power to judge. This combination of power effectively gave Deborah the same authority that would later be invested in the kings of Israel.

APPOINTED TO DO A NEW THING

Scripture does not reveal much about Deborah's early years. She seemingly burst onto the scene from a life of obscurity. No doubt she understood suffering, as she lived during the time when Israel spent twenty years under the iron-fisted rule of the

Canaanite king Jabin, during a time when barbaric practices of the Canaanite religion were commonplace.

PEOPLE HAVE A TENDENCY TO DRIFT

During Deborah's day, the entire nation of Israel drifted into something we see far too often in the Christian lifestyle: *compromise.*

Perhaps when people are taught that there are no right or wrong answers and that all individuals are gods unto themselves, they drift into the category of those who lose the willingness and ability to make valid, biblical value judgments.

> God intended His ordinances to bring life and to love people into His kingdom, not for them to serve as holier-than-thou judgments.

This happened when the people were allowed to do what was right in their own eyes (Deuteronomy 12:8). But that day ended when Israel entered Canaan and God's law was instituted. A standard of order was now set for people to walk in—to guide, guard, and protect people as opposed to legalistic usage of God's law to beat down and criticize the imperfect. Second Corinthians 3:6 teaches that religious legalism kills, "but the Spirit gives life." God intended His ordinances to bring life and to love people into His kingdom, not for them to serve as holier-than-thou judgments.

DEBORAH REMINDS ME OF SOMEONE

Time and again, God sent deliverance to Israel in unusual ways through unusual people. Deborah was one of them. I can imagine the people around her saying, "Are you kidding me? *She* can't possibly be our chosen leader."

But Deborah reminds me of Jesus. Israel had begun crying out for deliverance from the Canaanites. God heard and responded to their prayers of repentance and raised a deliverer from their midst. This deliverer was not a giant of a man like Samson. In fact, this deliverer was not a man at all, but a woman. Deborah, like Jesus, did not "look like" the rescuer Israel expected.

Israel was crying for deliverance from the Roman Empire when Jesus came, and He was not the type of deliverer the Pharisees were expecting. They anticipated a political leader who would deliver them from the bondage of Roman oppression.

Similarly, ancient Israel probably did not expect a woman to arise from their ranks to lead the nation. But Deborah did, perhaps not only to the shock and amazement of the nation, but perhaps to the amazement of Deborah herself.

IT WAS BUSINESS AS USUAL IN ISRAEL UNTIL GOD SPOKE TO DEBORAH

Deborah's courthouse was not an elaborate building; it was a palm tree situated in the mountains of Ephraim (Judges 4:5). How amazing, really, when we think of Deborah—esteemed judge in Israel, yet her office was a tree and heaven recorded her judgments.

Picture the everyday setting for this unique event. Deborah, Mrs. Lapidoth (Judges 4:4), was going about her business of administering justice when the Holy Spirit spoke to her.

> Now Deborah, a prophetess, the wife of Lapidoth, was judging Israel at this time. And she would sit under the palm tree of Deborah between Ramah and Bethel in the mountains of Ephraim. And the children of Israel came up to her for judgment. Then she sent and called for Barak the son of Abinoam from Kedesh in Naphtali, and said to him, "Has not the LORD God of Israel commanded, 'Go and deploy troops at Mount Tabor; take with you ten thousand men of the sons of Naphtali and of the sons of Zebulun; and against you I will deploy Sisera, the commander of Jabin's army, with his chariots and his multitude at the River Kishon; and I will deliver him into your hand'?" (Judges 4:4–7)

Deborah was minding her own business when the Holy Spirit spoke to her to deliver a military victory to Israel. Deborah did not rationalize this away. Scripture contains no record of her negotiating with God. Instead, she immediately responded in faith to her assignment. She called for Barak, the commanding general of the army of Israel.

Deborah did not yield to her weak military position, considering Israel had an infantry of only ten thousand soldiers enlisted at the time. Sisera, commander of the Canaanite army, had nine hundred chariots fit with iron to war against Israel, plus far more troops and cavalry.

The prophetess confidently told Barak that if they would deploy troops against Sisera, this pagan commander and his army would come out to fight and God would defeat them (Judges 4:6–7).

Deborah had heard the voice of God. Her faith was stirred, and she moved, fully expecting victory.

GENERAL BARAK'S AMAZING RESPONSE

I believe that Barak sensed God's anointing on Deborah's words. There is no biblical record that he was afraid to fight the Canaanites, but we do see in Judges 4:8 that he was absolutely unwilling to go to war without Deborah: "Barak said to her, 'If you will go with me, then I will go; but if you will not go with me, I will not go!'" He saw Deborah's strength, power, worth, and value, and because of that, he was not too proud to let her take the lead.

We learn three important lessons about Barak from his statement:

1. Barak believed prophecy to be a valid gift of God.
2. Barak obviously perceived Deborah to be a remarkable person, capable of hearing from God in a clear, distinct way.
3. Barak knew how to recognize that Deborah was operating under God's authority for a particular job and was willing to work with her.

We are living in an age when God is releasing in great measure the gifts of the Holy Spirit to His church and rewarding those who move in faith and respond to His prophetic instructions. God is consistent. He operated this way centuries ago through the birth of John the Baptist to Zacharias and Elizabeth. His birth was a direct result of a person who received a prophetic word (Luke 1:8–25).

Mary, the mother of Jesus, believed and received a prophetic word from the angel Gabriel that she would bear a son and call him Jesus (Luke 1:26–38). As believers, our lineage traced back to Jesus is a direct result of prophecy in the Gospels and all the way back to the book of Isaiah, when the prophet Isaiah spoke from the realm of the Spirit to foretell the birth of Jesus (Isaiah 7:14). We know from Amos 3:7 that God does nothing until He first reveals it to His prophets.

There is a resurgence in prophetic speaking today. Now, more than ever, we need to hear the true prophets speak, the wisdom of God to discern truth, and the courage to act on that truth.

A PROPHECY THAT WAS NOT WHAT IT SEEMED

The Holy Spirit again caused Deborah to prophesy to Barak: "I will surely go with you; nevertheless, there will be no glory for you in the journey you are taking, for the LORD will send Sisera into the hand of a woman" (Judges 4:9). The verse continues, "Then Deborah arose and went with Barak to Kedesh."

This passage makes me think more happened than is recorded. I wonder if there was a *What am I thinking, going to battle under a women's authority?* moment here. Did Barak

We are living in an age when God is releasing in great measure the gifts of the Holy Spirit to His church and rewarding those who move in faith and respond to His prophetic instructions.

suddenly begin thinking with his ego instead of listening to her words? In a moment of weakness, did he fail to see her gift in the Spirit and not hear what God had been saying through her? To me this represents a change, a double-mindedness, a move of the soul talking to him with a voice of fleshly reason over the voice of God.

Something caused Deborah to demonstrate that women could be in the role of authority and hear and obey God—and all the troops would benefit from it. But seemingly, she had to point out that being a woman did not diminish her God-ordained place of authority. God was making a point by showing the strength of a woman who would listen to Him and obey His voice even in battle.

Deborah allowed this situation to be a God thing, and in her strength, she displayed a godly character and nature that got the job done properly.

Deborah was not saying she would take the credit for winning the battle, but she did prophesy the results with amazing clarity: God can use whomever He chooses and whoever is willing to rise to the occasion.

VICTORY CAME AS GOD PROMISED

Then Deborah said to Barak, "Up! For this is the day in which the Lord has delivered Sisera into your hand. Has not the Lord gone out before you?" So Barak went down from Mount Tabor with ten thousand men following him. And the Lord routed Sisera and all his chariots and all his army with the edge of the sword before Barak; and Sisera alighted from his chariot and fled away on foot. But Barak pursued the chariots and the army as far as Harosheth Hagoyim, and all the army of Sisera fell by the edge of the sword; not a man was left. (Judges 4:14–16)

God routed the Canaanite army, and the Israelite army completely defeated their enemy. Then, as prophesied, General Sisera was delivered into the hands of a woman. Interestingly enough, that woman was not Deborah. She wasn't trying to gain glory or offend anyone. She was delivering the word of God to use a strategy He had designed to ensure the success of the mission.

We all have a position in God's kingdom. The authority God gives to one person does not diminish the authority someone else holds in his or her rightful position. It's all right—even beneficial to the kingdom—to find your seat of authority and be firmly fixed in it. From time to time, you may be called on to lead, follow, or stay in the car. Whatever God leads you to do, it is as He directs under proper authority from Him that the mission can succeed. In the story of Deborah and Barak, there weren't two leaders or two generals. Some led, some followed, but all succeeded when they were in proper order.

> It's not about sharing governance or sharing roles of authority. It's about listening to God to find each person's rightful place of authority so a mission can succeed.

It's not about sharing governance or sharing roles of authority. It's about listening to God to find each person's rightful place of authority so a mission can succeed. As God wins, every-body wins.

Women can be great leaders if they are great followers of God's Word. So can men and children. Leaders can be seen from the playground to the battleground, from the boardroom to the boardwalk. Great leadership comes from hearing the voice of God and obeying it not as a bully or out of arrogance, but as one submitted to His authority and to the success of His mission for His kingdom.

EVERY BATTLE IS DIFFERENT

However, Sisera had fled away on foot to the tent of Jael, the wife of Heber the Kenite; for there was peace between Jabin king of Hazor and the house of Heber the Kenite. And Jael went out to meet Sisera, and said to him, "Turn aside, my lord, turn aside to me; do not fear." And when he had turned aside with her into the tent, she covered him with a blanket.

Then he said to her, "Please give me a little water to drink, for I am thirsty." So she opened a jug of milk, gave him a drink, and covered him. And he said to her, "Stand at the door of the tent, and if any man comes and inquires of you, and says, 'Is there any man here?' you shall say, 'No.'"

Then Jael, Heber's wife, took a tent peg and took a ham-mer in her hand, and went softly to him and drove the peg into his temple, and it went down into the ground; for he was fast asleep and weary. So he died. And then, as Barak pursued Sisera, Jael came out to meet him, and said to him, "Come, I will show you the man whom you seek. And when

We all have a position in God's kingdom. The authority God gives to one person does not diminish the authority someone holds in his or her rightful position. It's all right—even beneficial to the kingdom—to find your seat of authority and be firmly fixed in it.

he went into her tent, there lay Sisera, dead with the peg in his temple. (Judges 4:17–22)

I'm not in any way telling you to do this at home—or anywhere else! Let's keep this in context. This was Old Testament. This was war. The enemies of God were trying to wipe out the people of God, and God had given specific instructions for a specific battle. Every battle, every leader, every strategy is different.

Even from Old Testament to New Testament, the battles and weapons are different. Old Testament times (before the shed blood of Jesus) were quite different for the children of Israel. Since the death, burial, and resurrection of Christ, our fight as individual believers should be the good fight of our faith.

Yes, the nations of the world have military forces, and we hear about wars and rumors of wars (Matthew 24:6; Mark 13:7). Bible prophecies point to the things we see happening daily. But let's not confuse those with the individual battles to which God calls us to "fight the good fight of faith" to defeat the enemy Satan, the devil, the thief who comes "to steal, and to kill, and to destroy" (1 Timothy 6:12; John 10:10).

As individual believers and as the body of Christ, we fight with weapons of our faith, and our individual battles must come under the authority of the Holy Spirit and be fought according to His directions to see victory over the devil's attack in our lives.

DEBORAH: FOUR OBSERVATIONS

1. Deborah did not bow to other people's opinions if their opinions did not reflect God's opinion.

2. Deborah did not consider her circumstances.
3. Deborah refused to be moved by the overwhelming odds against her.
4. Deborah was quick to honor the Lord God who had enabled her to do exploits through His name.

We all can draw upon Deborah's example as an overcomer. The same God who empowered her can empower every woman who hears His voice. Staying in faith and not accepting the negative opinions of others as our own may not be easy, but as Deborah demonstrated here, it is highly productive. God can have great vessels to work through for His glory as we keep our eyes on Him instead of on the challenges we face.

10

BITTER, BETTER, OR SWEET REVENGE?

I'd rather leave out this chapter altogether. It's about Mark 11, and frankly, there are days I actually wish the Bible had left out this chapter. But that's not the way it is. In my heart of hearts, I know how important it is for us as followers of Jesus to understand and consider Mark 11:22–25:

> Jesus answered and said to them, "Have faith in God. For assuredly, I say to you, whoever says to this mountain, 'Be removed and be cast into the sea,' and does not doubt in his heart, but believes that those things he says will be done, he will have whatever he says. Therefore I say to you, whatever things you ask when you pray, believe that you receive them, and you will have them. And whenever you stand praying, if you have anything against anyone, forgive him, that your Father in heaven may also forgive you your trespasses."

Notice that this passage includes many interesting truths. It reminds us that we can speak the Word of God and that the things we say can come to pass. However, for the faith described in Mark 11:22–24 to work, there's a three-letter word at the beginning of verse 25 that is very important: "And."

The word *and* is a conjunction. Our grammar books tell us that a conjunction connects words, sentences, or clauses to make a whole unit. For example, when you eat a peanut butter sandwich, you don't think of the bread and peanut butter separately. It's not just bread and not just peanut butter individually. It's bread *and* peanut butter joined together as a unit that makes the sandwich taste good! The same is true with Mark 11:22–24 and Mark 11:25. They must be joined together to work properly. This technically means we cannot get the first part of the passage about faith (vv. 22–24) to come to pass without also completing the second part—the forgiveness part (v. 25). Jesus connects forgiveness to faith—even if we don't want them to connect!

I had to face this scripture in order to move forward and do all God wanted me to do. In my own "human-ness," I honestly thought this was impossible. Let me explain why.

In another chapter, I talk about the man who asked a very insensitive question when my child died: "What do you think of your Jesus now that your son is dead?" There is more. As I was about to put my son's body into the ground, a woman came up to me and bluntly stated, "I prayed for your baby to die, and God answered my prayers." I am not kidding! *Someone actually said that.* So for me, moving forward and actually forgiving was extremely hard.

While very few people have been in my specific situation, I can imagine that you have had pain in your life because of people who have hurt you. So, whatever the circumstances of your life are, or have been, I'm here to tell you there's hope for you. I have shared my story to encourage your faith so that you can recover from deep anguish and move mountains in Jesus' name. Mark 11:25 truly does contain the key to unlocking that kind of faith.

THAT'S AN UNFAIR QUESTION

Against the backdrop of the memory of unfortunate encounters with people about my son's death, the Lord began to deal with me about forgiveness. I remember the Lord asking me a very interesting question, *Do you think I could forgive the people who hurt you?* I replied, "Yes, Lord, You can."

The Lord asked me if I believed Philippians 4:13, which says, "I can do all things through Christ who strengthens me." When I answered yes, He asked me another question. This one hit me deep in my heart: *If you think you can't forgive them, are you willing to hand them over to Me and forgive them through Christ who will give you the strength?* Because I was replaying my horrific memory in my head, my first response was, "That's an unfair question!" I came face-to-face with pain and anger and other emotions that I cannot even put into words. I had a choice to make: forgive or not forgive. Period.

In my years of ministry, I have had to deal with some of the worst people I possibly could have imagined. The worst part was that some of them even called themselves Christians, which made it even more difficult, more perplexing. But God did not put any qualifiers on Mark 11:25 when He said we have to forgive. It is a command—one of those "you do this thing, and then I will respond" kind of things. God required me to forgive so that He could release me into all Mark 11:22–25 had for me. This was clear. When I stood praying, I not only had to speak to the mountain of difficulty I was facing, but I had to believe in my heart and not doubt, *and* I had to choose to forgive. It was my choice.

During this experience, I looked at some of my preaching notes from 1991. I said that holding on to bitterness was like drinking poison and expecting the other person to die. That wasn't fair! These were my own notes, and I could not escape them. When I held on to bitterness, I was the one drinking the poison (metaphorically speaking), and I was the one feeling its effects.

The funny thing is, in 1991, when the Lord showed me that very practical truth about bitterness and unforgiveness, I was going through a trial, but it wasn't yet the biggest trial and test. It was just the beginning.

DECISION TIME

Once again, it was decision time for me. I learned from my father-in-law that I could make bitterness a part of my life, or I could let it go. If I released it to God, He was more than able to handle it and in a much wiser way than I ever could. Oral used to say that bitterness can lead to vengeance and vengeance can lead to revenge, and the whole vicious cycle is not worth messing with.

That does not mean in any way that an offense or a wound someone inflicts on us doesn't hurt or that it never happened.

God let me know that in some situations I faced, other people's actions were despicable. But even the despicable ones were offenses I needed to release so that He could handle them.

My forgiving the person had nothing to do with their actions. Keep in mind that Ephesians 6:12 says that we don't wrestle against flesh and blood (people), "but against principalities, against powers, against the rulers of the darkness of this age, against spiritual hosts of wickedness in the heavenly places."

Knowing that the person I was dealing with was not my problem made me feel a little bit better about the situation. You see, behind every situation was a power, a principality, or a ruler of darkness. Actually, it was a spiritual wickedness that came from the devil himself. Satan often uses people to carry out his plans. As a believer, my battles are not against people but against the evil power behind their words and actions. As a follower of Jesus, the most important fight I need to engage in is the good fight of my faith (1 Timothy 6:12).

The Lord led me to draw a line down the center of a sheet of paper. On one side of that line, He told me to put the names of the people who were causing me grief. On the other side, I wrote the actions they had taken to hurt or damage me. He then said to tear the paper in half and to look at the side that included painful actions taken against me. He said to me, *These actions are despicable, but they are for Me to deal with.* On the other side, however, I needed to look past the names of people who had wounded or offended me to see how the devil had worked through them. The Lord was wanting me to come against the devil, not the individuals involved. That way He could take care of each painful situation.

THE RECOMPENSE OF REWARD

The Lord then reminded me of Romans 12:19: "'Vengeance is Mine, I will repay,' says the Lord." As I studied this verse, I recognized that *vengeance* is the fight that belongs to God, and He would repay. The word *repay* means to compensate or recompense, and according to Strong's,[1] it is the same word in Hebrews 10:35 that says "recompence of reward" (KJV). It also means payment due in return for anything done or suffered.

This understanding of the word *repay* gave me such freedom. I could see that if I would release the people, forgive them, and turn them over to the Lord, not only would He take care of the situation and deal with those involved, but then He would repay me. That meant that I did not have to look to the people who wronged me or to anyone else to correct the injustice. In fact, He said, *I will compensate you with the recompense of My reward.*

Let's make this personal for you. Consider taking a step toward freedom, wholeness, and happiness by releasing any bitterness or unforgiveness you may hold. Not only can the Lord take care of anything wrong that has been done against you, but He can also heal your suffering and deal with the person or persons who caused it.

Many times when you're dealing with people who have hurt you, they not only don't care that you suffered; they may not even be aware that you suffered. Unless you bring it to their attention, it's entirely possible that they are clueless as to what happened. Romans 12:19 is one of the most freeing verses in the entire Bible.

FATHER, FORGIVE THEM

Releasing forgiveness to a person who doesn't deserve it is simply being like Jesus when on the cross He asked the Father to forgive. Jesus, sinless and blameless, went to the cross for sins He did not commit. In the middle of that injustice, He taught us about forgiveness.

People can cooperate with the devil and allow him to work through them so much or for so long that they don't even realize what they're doing. But that didn't matter to Jesus when He said, "Father, forgive them, for they do not know what they do" (Luke 23:34).

Forgiveness was not approving of the actions of those who hurt me, nor did it lessen the effect of the situation. It meant that I no longer had to carry the burden of what they had done, and Jesus could see something happening to me as a result of letting go of unforgiveness.

When God says that vengeance belongs to Him, He means it. He also says we are entitled to the recompense of reward. However, we can receive it only as we obey the whole Scripture by doing our part and putting confidence in God to do what He says He will do. So don't cast away your cheerful courage, boldness, and assurance in God, for He says in His Word that His desire is for you to receive payment due in return for anything given, done, or suffered (Hebrews 10:35).

GOD REPAYS

If we take God at His Word, bitter revenge becomes the sweet recompense of reward. You also can release yourself into all that God has for you. The sweet revenge of God is that He repays.

The revenge of human beings can be vile and vicious, and it brings messy consequences. But as we are willing to release to God the things we've suffered and demonstrate through acts of faith that we trust Him and take Him at His Word, believing that He is more than able to take care of our situations and us, this can become a turning point in our lives so that God can handle offenses on our behalf.

In the situation I've shared in this chapter, trust came to me when I believed that God could take care of it. As a recompense of reward, I get to stay in sweet fellowship with the Lord and not lose my peace. He not only took care of the other person and their deeds, but I didn't have to get my hands dirty in the process. Furthermore, God repaid me what was due me. When God takes care of the tab, when God repays, when God gives us the recompense of reward, we need to believe we have been rewarded. As Moses told the Israelites, "The Lord will fight for you, and you shall hold your peace" (Exodus 14:14).

THE LORD WILL FIGHT FOR YOU, AND YOU SHALL ACT LIKE A LADY

I actually wrote a little note in the margin of my Bible beside Exodus 14:14 that says, "The Lord will fight for me, and I shall act like a lady!" No matter what happens in our lives, we don't have to lose our peace. We don't have to lose anything if we allow the Lord to fight the battles that belong to Him in the first place.

If we will give God our vengeance, bitterness, unforgiveness, and all the negative emotions that go along with those things and allow Him to fight our battles, we can hold our peace.

Our job is to fight the good fight of our faith. I admit, sometimes it takes faith to say, "I can do all things through Christ who strengthens me" (Philippians 4:13). In my own strength, I'm sometimes not sure if I can forgive freely. But if I believe the Word and take Jesus at His Word, then as an act of faith, I really can forgive through Christ who gives me the strength to do it.

> "The Lord will fight for me, and I shall act like a lady!"

CONSIDER FORGIVING

Consider forgiving by faith. Consider turning those wounded, damaged, unfair places in your life over to the Lord. Consider setting yourself free from anything that would give the devil the upper hand in the category of bitterness or unforgiveness.

As an act of your faith in the Lord, release it, give it to Him, and pray now:

> *Lord, this situation is for You to deal with. And because of that, I am asking You for the recompense of reward. I thank You, Father God, that You hear and answer my prayer. I declare myself free from every situation that has*

caused unforgiveness. This prayer doesn't change what happened to me, but by releasing the person who created the offense, I can now hold on to Your recompense of reward. And I thank You in advance for repaying all that You have for me.

In Jesus' name, amen.

EVELYN ROBERTS:
AN UNFORGETTABLE
WOMAN OF KINDNESS

Over the years, I have been privileged to know some women God has used in amazing ways. They come from different walks of life and embraced different callings, but no matter their differences, they have all shared a great love for and dedication to our Savior. Among these women, the one with whom I was privileged to share the closest relationship was my remarkable mother-in-law, Evelyn Lutman Roberts. You may or may not know much about her, and I hope that my sharing her with you in this chapter will help you become familiar with her so that her life will inspire you.

If Deborah was the honeybee, then Evelyn Roberts was the *queen bee,* and we all knew it. Oral used to say that he was the head of his household, but Evelyn was the neck that turns the head. Then he would laugh and laugh—perhaps because he knew the truth in that statement! Oral always referred to her as "my darling wife, Evelyn." Personally, I think she should have been called his "very balanced, exceedingly stable, grounding, safety-net, darling wife, Evelyn."

Richard and I used to say that Oral was the high flyer, the tightrope walker, the one so far out on the trapeze that only God could catch him. In contrast, Evelyn's feet were so firmly planted on the ground, so safe, secure, and immovable, that Oral knew he would be all right as long as he had her. She was the safety net, the glue, the grounding wire of his life. Her world revolved around her family and primarily around her husband, yet she never lost herself. Her grandchildren referred to her as "Munna," and it was music to her ears. She spent her entire adult life as the wife, mother, grandmother, and great-grandmother of someone, and she flourished in those roles.

> Evelyn's world revolved around her family and primarily around her husband, yet she never lost herself.

Evelyn's journey started on April 22, 1917, in Missouri, but somewhere along the way, Evelyn Lutman met a tall, handsome Cherokee Indian preacher named Oral Roberts. On that night, she wrote in her diary that she had met the man she would someday marry.

When Evelyn and Oral met, she was a schoolteacher, and he was, well—Oral! Even his name means "spoken word." And did he ever have a way with spoken words! After a short but sweet courtship, he asked her to marry him by proclaiming,

Evelyn, my huge, happy, hilarious heart is throbbing tumultuously, tremendously, triumphantly with a lingering, lasting, long-lived love for you. As I gaze into your bewildering, beauteous, bounteous, beaming eyes, I am literally, lonesomely lost in a dazzling, daring, delightful dream in which your fair, felicitous, fanciful face is ever present like a colossal, comprehensive constellation. Will you be my sweet, smiling, soulful, satisfied spouse?

Evelyn replied, "Listen here, Oral, if you are trying to propose to me, speak in the English language!" He did. She said yes, and they were married on Christmas Day 1938.

More than anyone I have ever known, Evelyn knew how to live a life of unconventionality. She had to, as her husband was often away from home, dreamed big, and spent much of his life traveling to bring God's love to the nations of the earth. She knew Oral was a gift. Even if he was gone and her children were hurting or the plumbing was a mess or something else had gone wrong, she was the woman for the job. She let Oral be himself and always knew her place, but she *was* the queen bee. While also staying true to herself and strong in her own identity, she always managed to help Oral find himself and to assist him in everything he was called to do so he could be all he was called to be.

A WOMAN OF WISDOM

Evelyn had an uncanny knack for knowing what to say and when to say it—and when to say nothing at all. Wisdom is required for knowing when to speak up and when to stay quiet. The book of Ecclesiastes says it this way: "To everything there is a season, a time for every purpose under heaven . . . a time to keep silence, and a time to speak" (3:1, 7). Is it best to step forward or step back, or make a way for someone else? No matter what position we find ourselves in to accomplish a certain task, it takes wisdom to know when to graciously submit to someone else's gifting and when to assume the role as leader.

> Wisdom is required for knowing when to speak up and when to stay quiet.

Evelyn Roberts was a great example of that wisdom. Perhaps the best and certainly the most memorable illustration of her wisdom was when she prepared to tape television shows. Everyone involved could count on her hair, her makeup, her clothes—everything needed for the job—to be in perfect order. Her nails were always perfect, and from the day I met her until she went home to heaven twenty-five years later, she wore the same color nail polish. She was always impeccably put together and always on time. Never early and never ever, *ever* late.

Wherever she was, whatever the job called for, that's what she did—smile or be appropriately somber, talk or not talk, sit or stand. Whatever the occasion required, she knew how to handle it. She was all business, very professional. She was a perfect match for Oral, who in my opinion, had his feet on earth but his heart and mind in heaven. He paid little attention to time and space but knew much about God and obedience to Him.

Oral was the healing evangelist known as the "Something Good" man with handsome Cherokee features, who loved to dress up, dapper and stylish, until the day he went home to be with Jesus.

Oral was the idea man who, in the twinkling of an eye, could change everything the people around him had spent months working on—and he expected them to carry out those changes in minutes (or seconds). He knew that every minute and every second meant a precious life could be saved, healed, or delivered for the kingdom of God.

Oral was consumed with a relentless focus on doing whatever it took to get someone suffering to meet the healing Jesus. On one memorable taping day, Oral had decided to have a candle-lighting service to pray for his precious partner family, a true family that meant the world to him.

That day we set a beautiful table with candles as Oral had requested and gave him thousands of prayer requests to pray for. Why the candles? I don't know. I just knew it was a bad idea from the start. When dealing with fire, the risks are high!

When I say Oral was serious about praying for his partners, I mean it. As he picked up each stack of prayer requests, he closed his eyes, held them in his hands, and literally hugged them to his chest. However, somehow during that particular prayer time he managed to lean forward into the candles and set the entire stack of prayer sheets on fire. *On fire.* He was so focused on his prayer that he didn't notice the flames. Typical Oral.

Not wanting to interrupt this time of prayer, the rest of us in the room were not sure what to do, which was typical of us. But instantly, dear Evelyn jumped up, took matters into her own hands, and began beating the flames out with the rest of the prayer sheets. Typical Evelyn, always thoroughly prepared for

Oral. Meanwhile our staff grabbed nearby fire extinguishers and began putting out the flames, until Oral finally looked up at us perplexed and asked, "What are you doing?"

Needless to say, the prayer sheets were well prayed over! We were relieved that Oral didn't set his hair on fire and not surprised that Evelyn handled the emergency calmly and effectively. Teamwork. Queen Bee, woman God could use, Evelyn.

RICE PILAF RELATIONSHIPS

Any friendship that lasts for more than sixty years is certainly remarkable. And the stories resulting from the friendship between Oral and Evelyn Roberts and Demos and Rose Shakarian (Demos founded the Full Gospel Business Men's Fellowship International) could fill volumes. The joy they experienced together, the conversations they enjoyed, and the recipes they shared were epic, to say the least.

Both Evelyn Roberts and Rose Shakarian had husbands whose ministries spanned the globe, yet all four of these friends came from humble beginnings. But what most people never realized was that one of the highlights of their relationship centered around rice. Yes, rice.

The story began when I fell in love with a marvelous rice dish that Evelyn served on special occasions. It was a favorite of Oral's and a favorite of everyone she served it to. She served it in a lovely dish with beautiful silverware, making it appear very special, so those gathered around the table felt blessed to feast on this "creation."

The comedy was revealed to me when I asked Evelyn for the recipe. "I really hate to give out the recipe," she admitted. I thought she was reluctant to share it because she and Rose held it as their friendship secret. But the truth was that the rice casserole we all marveled over was nothing more than instant rice and a box of dry, packaged chicken soup mix. I don't think I ever heard her laugh so hard as when she confided her prized recipe to me. She told me there were no painstaking hours spent in the kitchen and no special technique or fancy ingredient to be passed on in a recipe to children or grandchildren. So simple yet so amazing.

I truly believe the secret ingredient of Evelyn's delicious rice pilaf was love. Pure love. She prepared it, presented it, and described it as the secret recipe passed down from Rose to her beloved friend Evelyn with such great love people just knew it was special. The years of this rice pilaf relationship were more precious than gold—all because of a packet of seasoning.

Evelyn made that dish for us many, many times over many years. Of course, I made it for Oral and Evelyn for many years after I learned the recipe. But the best part of the dish was when Evelyn would talk about friendship and love and the simplicity of the Roberts's wonderful relationship with the Shakarians. And she would compare it to our relationship with God.

She talked about how simple it is to know God because God is always wrapped around love. Just as her sweet serving dish and her special recipe always made others feel special at any given moment, she would talk about how God wanted us to feel special in the same way. If any reflection of God can be seen through Evelyn and her rice, it's that of love. Pure love.

EVELYN AND GOD

Evelyn had always wanted to be a missionary to the world. She once called me and said she was "fuming mad," as angry as she could be, having just finished a conversation with God about Oral. I thought, *Oh dear, what could Oral have possibly done now?*

Evelyn was never angry. She simply dealt with problems as they arose. Upset? Mad? Never! So she had my curiosity at an all-time high. I couldn't wait to hear what she had to say. All I could think was, *Oral's gonna get it!*

Oral often did things simply to try to upset Evelyn, and he had it down to an art form. His favorite game of "Let's frustrate Evelyn" usually involved breaking something. He loved to lean back on every chair in the house just to see what she would do. It often ended badly, with Oral on the floor asking for help, chair leg broken, and Evelyn walking away, saying, "Now, Oral, I told you not to do that." No help. No sympathy.

Every time we heard those two words, "Now, Oral," we would know we were about to be entertained and ran to see what was happening. Evelyn kept Oral human, down to earth, and real. We all put him on a spiritual pedestal in the right perspective and honored him as God's servant. Evelyn did, too, more than anyone did. But she also kept him real. "Now, Oral," was such a familiar phrase in our household that our children learned to join in, saying, "Now, Oral," on their way to watch what was unfolding. He had no chance for mercy when "Now, Oral" came out of Evelyn's mouth.

Like a child with his hand in the cookie jar, he was caught. No excuses. And we all knew and loved it. "Now, Oral" may have been two of the sweetest words ever spoken. To this day, with Oral and Evelyn both in heaven, when something silly happens in our family, we break out in laughter and begin explaining by saying, "Now, Oral."

But let's get back to my story. When Evelyn said she was upset, I had to hear about it in person. When I arrived at her house, I could tell this was different—not just another "Now, Oral" moment. That day she told me she felt insignificant to God and to the world compared to him. She had always wanted to be a missionary and travel to the nations and win people to Jesus. Oral, however, wanted to be the governor of Oklahoma, and there he was traveling the nations of the world, having unglamorous experiences in difficult situations, but being very fulfilled in all of them. Evelyn, however, did not feel that she was contributing enough to God or to the world.

That day she asked God to speak to her or use her in some great way as He used Oral. But God said, *No, that's for Oral.* She was hurt at first and almost upset with God, which made me laugh out loud. When normal people are upset, it's like a 10 on the angry chart. With Evelyn, it was like a .001, so from my perspective, it never really counted as being angry.

When I asked her what happened next, she said the Lord was so sweet in His response to her. He said, *I will speak to you in the everydayness of life.* And how God genuinely did use her in the everydayness of life! How He spoke to her in His still, small voice in the little things, in everyday life situations with everyday people. What an impact she had on people every day.

WHERE IS THE RAPTURE
WHEN YOU NEED IT?

Perhaps the most unusual experience I ever had concerning my mother-in-law also involves the word *bittersweet*. Evelyn's homegoing was one of the hardest things I've ever experienced. At the same time, it was perhaps one of the sweetest situations I was ever involved in with my father-in-law, Oral.

In typical Evelyn Roberts fashion, she gave me years in advance strict instructions and detailed notes regarding her desires for her homegoing celebration. For some reason, when she shared her wishes, I never really thought that I would have to deal with that day. I don't know, maybe I thought the rapture or something different would happen. But it didn't.

So when Evelyn moved from earth to heaven, there I was with the task of carrying out the details she had given to me years earlier. As I had promised her, I would carry out each request exactly as she wanted. I never dreamed how grueling this task would actually be.

Throughout the planning of the service, Oral insisted that he could not speak because it would be too difficult for him. Evelyn had talked about that with me as well. In the event that she predeceased him, she wanted Oral to do whatever he wanted to do, but she thought speaking would be too difficult for him. I agreed with that, told him that everything was in place, and let him know that he did not have to talk if he did not want to.

As the time for the service drew near, he asked me to sit next to him in the car that would take us to the service. Every fiber of my soul wanted desperately to say no. I had no idea what

I would say or do. I was trying to be a strong person for Richard, yet this was my precious father-in-law, and I could see how he was suffering. I finally agreed to sit next to him, and on the way to the service, I asked if he was okay. I realize now what a ridiculous question that was, but I was at such a loss for words. This man who had represented a rock of healing for me since I was twelve years old now looked so broken to me.

He could have said by faith that he was doing great. I'm all for faith, really, but I had to sit next to him in the car and look at his face as he answered my question. He looked directly at me and said, "Tell me what I'm going to do now."

I said, "Well, you don't have to speak. You don't have to do anything. Just sit next to us, and we will get through this together."

He responded, "No, I mean in life. What am I going to do now?"

Needless to say, I had absolutely no answer to that question. So I did what I always did when I was with Oral: I spoke truthfully. Good or bad, happy or sad, he always knew that I would tell him the truth. I said that I had no idea what he was going to do or what the rest of us were going to do, but that I believed God would get us through it.

He looked straight at me and asked, "Do you really?"

I think that was the hardest question I've ever had to answer in my entire life, but I dug deep and said that I did indeed believe God would carry us through. Oral simply said, "Well, then you're going to have to help me."

And I said, "Okay." We said nothing else until we arrived at the service. The silence was intense—the air in the car was heavy. There was the person I had looked up to after my father died when I was twelve because he said something good was going to happen to me. I turned on the television every Sunday just to hear him say those words. Now there I was, years later, telling him we could get through this together. Talk about seed faith. I never dreamed that the seeds of prayer he poured into twelve-year-old Lindsay in Michigan—a girl he'd never met— would turn into this. I had an amazing opportunity to give back to him. Isn't that just like God?

With other family members, Richard and I walked into the service. So many people—extended family, friends, ministry colleagues—came together to give honor to such a worthy woman. What an amazing sight.

As the service was about to start, Oral looked at Richard and said, "I need to speak. I *want* to do this." Richard arranged for a time slot he felt would be appropriate. And, oh my, did he ever get up and talk. He poured out his heart and soul and did the most phenomenal job any of us ever could have imagined. He did not present as a broken shell of a man, but as God's man with the power of God all over him, standing up at the hardest time in his life, in front of thousands of people, to give the sweetest honor to Evelyn.

On the way home, I told Oral how proud I was of him. There had been no big fanfare as there was when he preached at crusades to thousands and thousands of people in the big tents. No television audience. Just Richard and me sharing from our hearts, telling him how proud we were of him. During the car ride home, he told me that in the following weeks he wanted to meet with me and plan his homegoing service, exactly as I had done for Evelyn. Then he said the most shocking thing he had ever said to me. Amazingly, he said he felt his life could never compare with Evelyn's, but that he still wanted to plan his service, just like she did.

I was so touched. Here was Oral Roberts saying that his life could never compare with Evelyn's life. Wow! Only heaven will tell the greatness of some people who live a quiet life behind the scenes, as Evelyn did. God already knew of Evelyn's greatness. But I believe everyone in the service recognized it on that day. And perhaps what would have been most important to Evelyn was that her precious Oral knew it.

Evelyn related to people everywhere, right where they were, where they hurt, and where they had need in the everydayness of their lives. From presidents to those in poverty, she was the same. She didn't move mountains. She simply touched hearts every day. She was a cornerstone, a queen bee woman all day every day until she went to heaven, leaving a tremendous legacy of profound power and influence in the everydayness of life here on earth.

> Evelyn simply touched hearts every day.

BYKOTA

And be ye kind one to another, tenderhearted, forgiving one another, even as God for Christ's sake hath forgiven you. (Ephesians 4:32 KJV)

As a mother, I taught my children this scripture by using the acronym BYKOTA: Be Ye Kind One to Another. I did my best to *teach* my children this scripture. But Evelyn did her best to *live* it. If ever there was a human being who had a good—really great—reason to be bitter or hateful toward people, it was Evelyn. From the media to total strangers and even some fellow Christians, Evelyn experienced the good, the bad, the very ugly, and even the very unbelievable. Yet, it never changed her. If anything, she changed those situations. She never really "killed" anyone with kindness, but she certainly diffused many encounters that could have turned toxic had someone else been handling them. She was a genuinely kind person, and why some people chose to hate her kindness will forever be a mystery to me.

One of the greatest examples of this happened when I took Evelyn to church one Sunday. Yes, in church. We sat near the front and center where it was hard to miss her. It was painfully obvious that the pastor knew exactly who she was. Yet he proceeded to preach with "snarky" (wow, I put that kindly!) anti–Oral Roberts comments the entire time. I was new to this *anti* talk from the pulpit and was honestly shocked to hear it in church. But I'm sure it was not a first for my mother-in-law.

As soon as the service was dismissed, we made our way toward the exit but were unable to avoid the whole "shake hands with the pastor" route out of the church. *Now what?* I wondered.

Well, Evelyn was Evelyn. In her unwavering kindness, she held out her hand and complimented the pastor (who tried to look the other way) on the good points of his message. Me, not so much. I was not accustomed to such public negativity toward Oral with Evelyn sitting in the congregation, and it was difficult to watch to say the least.

When the two of us got in the car, not one word was said about what had happened. Not. One. Word. I doubt very seriously that the pastor had any idea that he was in the presence of greatness, a woman of great kindness, that day. He may not have realized it, but I certainly did. I not only realized it, but to this day I have not forgotten it. "Be ye kind one to another." It's not just a scripture and a good idea. It's a lifestyle, an Evelyn Roberts kind of lifestyle from which we all can learn.

LET'S LEARN FROM EVELYN'S EXAMPLE

Can Evelyn's remarkable impact on ordinary life be duplicated? Absolutely not. But all of us can learn from it. How did Evelyn become a significant force for good without a traditional platform or microphone? Simple. She loved God with all her heart and selflessly did all she could to introduce everyone she could to the God she loved so much. Can there ever be another Evelyn? No. But can there be another woman who can become all the things God declares and do all that God asks her to do? Absolutely! An Evelyn Roberts–style woman God can use mightily. Difficult but not impossible. I've been working on it for years.

Now that you have gained a glimpse into the life of a remarkable modern-day woman God can use, a woman of true worth, I hope and pray the lessons she taught me and the life I saw her live will inspire you. Just as she accepted the role God had assigned to her and flourished in it, I pray you will also embrace what He has called you to do—whether it's behind the scenes or on a stage, in a position of great influence or a place of deep impact on the people closest to you. Fame and numbers are not part of God's equation. All He's looking for—and what He rewards—is faithfulness to do what He has chosen and equipped you to do.

12

CRAZY, AMAZING MIRACLES

Based on the title of this chapter, you may be wondering, *What in the world is a crazy, amazing miracle, and what does it have to do with my true worth?* Good thing I didn't go with my other title option, which was "If Spit Would Bring Sight and Camels Would Walk and Women Would Cry." We'll explore each of these in this chapter, but for now, to help you understand what crazy, amazing miracles are, it's helpful to separate *crazy* and *amazing.*

When you think of the word *miracle*, a divine intervention from God, do you think it's crazy, or do you think it's amazing? I've noticed that when I talk about miracles, some people think the idea of miracles is crazy, while others think it's amazing.

I'm reminded of a story my father-in-law told me about President John F. Kennedy. Oral went to the White House to have a time of fellowship and prayer with him. Since this was Oral's first visit to the White House, he didn't know what to expect. But the president started the conversation by saying, "Oral, tell me about the miracles." To President Kennedy, miracles were not crazy; they were amazing.

But what do *you* believe? I've seen and experienced so many miracles throughout my lifetime that I can't even begin to doubt that God has miracles for each of us. As we stretch our faith, those miracles, signs, and wonders are just waiting for us to discover them.

What does this have to do with healed eyesight, camels, women's tears, and walking on water? It's *all* about miracles. Jesus is the miracle worker, and He said that according to our faith in Him, we would do greater works after He returned to heaven (John 14:12). Miracles were a part of His daily life on earth, and I believe He wants them to be a part of every believer's daily walk with Him. Let's consider several of the Bible's crazy, amazing miracles.

IF SPIT WOULD BRING SIGHT

In John 9 we read about an unusual encounter that took place in Jesus' ministry. When Jesus saw a blind man, He did one of the most unexpected things I've ever read in the Bible. I would definitely call it a crazy, amazing miracle, and it's one of many works Jesus performed that left the people around Him in awe. "He spit on the ground and made mud with the saliva. Then he anointed the man's eyes with the mud and said to him, 'Go, wash in the pool of Siloam' (which means Sent). Se he went and washed and came back seeing" (John 9:6–7 ESV).

Trying to find the source of the blindness instead of the source of the healing, the disciples started asking Jesus questions about who had sinned and caused this man's blindness (John 9:2). Jesus answered by saying that neither the man nor his parents had sinned, but that He would use this as an example of God's healing power to demonstrate God's love and to glorify God (John 9:3–5).

Jesus spit on the ground. *He just simply spit on the ground!* Can you imagine the reaction of the disciples or other onlookers? Can you imagine what they must have been thinking? Instead of making some grand gesture and saying something like, "Be healed in My name," or "Watch the power of God take place," or "See what My Father God can do for you," Jesus simply spit on the ground.

The Bible says He combined the spit with the dirt and rubbed it on the man's eyes (John 9:6). Then He told the man to go wash in a nearby pool (v. 7). Now, I would have imagined something more dramatic when Jesus was talking to the blind man, wanting to heal him. I would have envisioned Jesus having a discussion with the man about how glorious the power of God is and how amazing the miracle would be. I certainly would have thought Jesus would engage in some form of conversation with the man to see if he believed in God or believed in the Son of God.

But none of that happened. To my surprise and perhaps to the surprise of those around him, this did not play out as I expected. Jesus spit on the ground, combined the dirt and the spit, and then placed the mud mixture on the man's eyes.

When I first read this story, it intrigued me. Why would Jesus behave like that? For the longest time my only takeaway was that Jesus picked up the mud from the ground, placed it on the man's eyes, and told him to go wash—and the man was healed.

When the man was asked to describe what had happened, he simply said, "The man called Jesus made mud and anointed my eyes and said to me, 'Go to Siloam and wash.' So I went and washed and received my sight" (John 9:11 ESV). The man's brief account was good enough for me. For years that was the simple way I looked at the story. Eventually the Holy Spirit granted me some amazing insight about Jesus' spittle, the mud He used, and the miracle He performed. So allow me to share that with you.

According to dictionary.com, the definition of *spit* is "saliva, especially when ejected."[1] *Mud* is "wet, soft earth or earthy matter."[2]

A *miracle* is "an effect or extraordinary event in the physical world that surpasses all known human or natural powers and is ascribed to a supernatural cause." And "such an effect or event manifesting or considered as a work of God."[3]

DNA FROM JESUS

One day as I thought about the story of the blind man's healing, I read an article about family history and family genetics on the KQED website.[4] Something began to click regarding the spit, the mud, and the miracle. The article referred to DNA, our genetic coding. It connects us to our ancestors and our bloodline, and it even reveals illnesses to which we are predisposed.

The article said that if we put all our DNA molecules end to end, they would reach from the earth to the sun and back more than six hundred times. To put that into perspective, consider that it's ninety-three million miles to the sun. Human DNA *can stretch across that distance and back more than six hundred times!* As Psalm 139:14 says, we are "fearfully and wonderfully made."

As I continued reading the article, I discovered that the way to determine our DNA and get scientific information about our genetic coding is to have our spit analyzed. Our DNA and genetic code are found in our spit. If we couple that information with the fact that we are made from the dust or dirt of the earth, we gain new insight into John 9:6. The way I look at that scripture now is that Jesus spit to infuse *His* DNA into the dust of the earth—the dirt from which God made us. Jesus took the spit, the DNA that represented who He is, and mixed it with the dirt of the earth, representing who we are. The mud formed by the combination of the spit and the dirt performed the miracle in the man's eyes!

Since we are fearfully and wonderfully created by God, then why can't we be fearfully and wonderfully recreated when Jesus infuses the essence of who He is into the essence of who we are? First John 4:4 says, "You are of God, little children," and "He who is in you is greater than he who is in the world."

This means we are of God—born into His family, partakers of His nature, capable of reflecting His character. We are created in His image. And, through Jesus, we can share in God's own nature.

When we accept Jesus as our Savior, spiritually speaking we have the DNA and the genetic coding of our Father God. If we have the genetic origin of our Father God, we can live healed and whole. God is not sick. God is not confused. God is not depressed or poor. And since that's true, can't we live according to those blessings in every area of our lives? If Jesus did it, and we are to be like Jesus, can't we, by the genetic coding of our Father God through His Son Jesus Christ, be healed and made whole?

REALIZE THAT GOD'S POWER IS IN YOU

When we who have the power of Jesus on the inside of us dare to take the "spit"—the supernatural infusion of Jesus Christ within us—and combine it by faith with the "dust"—whatever it is that God has given us to use in the natural realm—we have a right to expect a miracle! As we mix the supernatural infusion of God with whatever is in our hand, our life, our substance, we can ask God to anoint it and breathe His supernatural breath of life into it to make a miracle. Consider your true worth as God's beloved child.

By this point in the book, I hope your belief in miracles has been stirred to an all-time high—not just for the things you may think of as miracles of biblical proportion, but also for the miracles you need in your everyday life. They are the breakthroughs you could never accomplish or experience in your own strength, the areas in which nothing will ever change until God Himself does something remarkable on your behalf. The miracle you need may seem impossible to other people, or it may seem so insignificant that they would ask, "Why would you call *that* a miracle?"

No miracle is too big for God, and no miracle is too small. Whether you are in the midst of a true crisis or are eleven dollars short on your rent payment, when you have a need you cannot meet for yourself—no matter how hard you try—it's time to get out of the mess you're in and into the miracle you need. Whatever that

> No miracle is too big for God, and no miracle is too small.

miracle is, the first step toward it is faith. When you become a woman of faith, when faith is the greatest force in your life, miracles can happen. I'm not just talking about *a* miracle; I'm talking about *your* miracle.

IF CAMELS COULD WALK ...

The queen of Sheba came to visit King Solomon, bearing much wealth (1 Kings 10:1–13). Who carried the wealth? The camels!

> Now when the queen of Sheba heard of the fame of Solomon concerning the name of the LORD, she came to test him with hard questions. She came to Jerusalem with a very great retinue, with camels that bore spices, very much gold, and precious stones; and when she came to Solomon, she spoke with him about all that was in her heart. So Solomon answered all her questions; there was nothing so difficult for the king that he could not explain it to her. And when the queen of Sheba had seen all the wisdom of Solomon, the house that he had built, the food on his table, the seating of his servants, the service of his waiters and their apparel, his cupbearers, and his entryway by which he went up to the house of the LORD, there was no more spirit in her. Then she said to the king: "It was a true report which I heard in my

own land about your words and your wisdom. However I did not believe the words until I came and saw with my own eyes; and indeed the half was not told me. Your wisdom and prosperity exceed the fame of which I heard. Happy are your men and happy are these your servants, who stand continually before you and hear your wisdom! Blessed be the LORD your God, who delighted in you, setting you on the throne of Israel! Because the LORD has loved Israel forever, therefore He made you king, to do justice and righteousness."

Then she gave the king one hundred and twenty talents of gold, spices in great quantity, and precious stones. There never again came such abundance of spices as the queen of Sheba gave to King Solomon. Also, the ships of Hiram, which brought gold from Ophir, brought great quantities of almug wood and precious stones from Ophir. And the king made steps of the almug wood for the house of the LORD and for the king's house, also harps and stringed instruments for singers. There never again came such almug wood, nor has the like been seen to this day.

Now King Solomon gave the queen of Sheba all she desired, whatever she asked, besides what Solomon had given her according to the royal generosity. So she turned and went to her own country, she and her servants. (1 Kings 10:1–13)

The queen of Sheba was so impressed when she heard about Solomon's wealth, wisdom, and overall kingdom experience that she came to see him. She loaded a caravan of camels with provisions so extravagant that the Bible records the details. The camels were carrying gold, spices, precious stones, and no telling what else. Why? Because she had heard of Solomon's fame and knew of his relationship with God because of his position as Israel's king, and she wanted to come and find answers to some hard questions.

Let's not miss something important here. Solomon was already the richest man at this time in history, so why did the queen take such extravagant gifts to him? The answer has two parts. First, she wanted some of his wisdom, so she did not want to approach him empty-handed. So often we see people who want something for nothing. But etiquette tells us not to visit people with our hands empty. Always take a hostess gift to the party. How many times have I shared this principle with my daughters: when you're receiving from what someone else has, sow out of what you have. And look what the queen of Sheba received! King Solomon gave her "all she desired" (1 Kings 10:13). Can you imagine being taught by the wisest man in the world?

Second, Solomon wasn't a show-off who bragged about his greatness or spread his own fame throughout the land. He was developing a relationship with God and worshiping Him. At the temple dedication described a couple of chapters earlier, Solomon had said, "May these words of mine, with which I have made supplication before the LORD, be near the LORD our God day and night . . . that all the peoples of the earth may know that the LORD is God; there is no other" (1 Kings 8:59–60). God honored him for that.

So here came the queen of Sheba with her caravan of gifts. Seriously, a *caravan* of gifts, including gold, spices, and precious stones. Who does that? A person so hungry to receive that she is willing to give her best.

In 1 Kings 10:4–5 we read that when the queen saw the

vastness of Solomon's kingdom and his possessions, there was no more breath or spirit in her. Perhaps today we would say she was so overwhelmed that it took her breath away. Maybe she even fainted!

For me the most important point in this story is that Solomon had never asked for the camels or the gifts they carried. He simply developed his relationship with God. As he did, God let the word spread to Sheba (1 Kings 8:60), and the queen of Sheba told the camels to start walking.

As we focus on our relationship with God, the camels of provision can start walking. As we seek first the kingdom of God and His ways of operating in the kingdom (in other words, how we are to be obedient to His Word), everything we need will be added to us (Matthew 6:33).

AND WOMEN WOULD CRY . . .

Turning to the New Testament, we read in Mark 5:25–34 about the woman with the flow of blood who reached out to Jesus and touched His garment. Jesus felt the healing power flow from Him into someone. Since a huge crowd was surrounding Him, He asked, "Who touched My clothes?" (v. 30). The disciples said, "You see the multitude thronging You, and You say, 'Who touched Me?'" (v. 31). They were basically saying, "Everyone wants to touch you, Lord." But Jesus knew that something about that woman's touch was different from any other touch. This was a touch of faith believing for healing power from Him. The woman told Him her whole story (v. 33), and He said to her, "Daughter, your faith has made you well. Go in peace, and

Jesus has
always been
attracted
to faith.

be healed of your affliction" (v. 34). Jesus contained the healing power of God, but the woman's faith "magnetized" it out of Him.

Magnets are interesting. They operate with a push-pull force. Something attracts and draws out. The north ends of two magnets or the south ends of two magnets repel each other. But a north and a south end of two magnets attract. Jesus has always been attracted to faith. This wasn't about His faith and her faith or His power and her power. This is the story of her faith *and* His power. The woman's faith magnetized Jesus' healing power and drew it to her, and nothing could stop that from happening.

God honors faith and "shows no partiality" (Acts 10:34). When we stretch out our faith, believing in His miraculous power, how can that power be stopped? God has to honor His Word.

Your faith is of great worth!

13

BECOMING A WOMAN
OF FAITH

In chapter 12 we talked about our "mud." The mud that God uses to perform a miracle symbolizes the natural aspects of our lives, the things we offer Him to use as He chooses. In this chapter I want to focus on one of those natural gifts—the gift of speaking. Our words are more powerful than we may realize. When we combine our words with our faith in God, amazing things happen.

For years many of us have heard about the importance of speaking words of faith. Sometimes people think that speaking words of faith is more important than believing them. I don't believe that to be true. Faith and speaking go hand in hand. When we want to see God move, we *first* believe, and *then* we speak. Our words must be directly related to our faith.

TALK IS CHEAP, BUT OH, MY WORD!

"Out of the abundance of the heart" the mouth speaks (Luke 6:45). "Death and life are in the power of the tongue, and those who love it will eat its fruit" (Proverbs 18:21). And as a person thinks in his own heart, so he becomes (Proverbs 23:7). This becomes the pattern as you think a thought and then believe it in your heart. Then, from your heart, as you have agreed or disagreed with that thought, you speak it out of your mouth. Those words become so powerful that God must honor them as you have believed.

Now let's put these scriptures pertaining to words into perspective according to 3 John 2: "Beloved, I pray that you may prosper in all things and be in health, just as your soul prospers." The soul is comprised of the mind, the will, and the emotions. As we get those in order, we can prosper and be in health in every other area of our lives.

The words *just as* mean "just as, in the same proportion as, in the degree that, in as much as."[1] One is totally dependent on the other. At the same proportional rate your soul prospers, you are to prosper and be in health, according to the Scripture. But if your soul (your mind, will, and emotions) believes the wrong thing, then how can any other area prosper? If any area is out of sync, all become out of sync. Everything is tied together. Therefore, our words become vitally important for us to prosper in all areas as a whole person. And isn't being whole so much better than being fragmented and torn apart into little pieces? Again, our words affect that outcome.

I believe one of the main reasons we do not live in the fullness of everything God has for us—in our true worth—is that we sabotage our success with the words we speak. It's one thing to hear something and think about it; it's another thing to believe it and speak it. As I mentioned earlier, Proverbs 23:7 tells us that as a person "thinks in his heart, so is he." In other words, as we think in our hearts and speak out of our mouths, we will become what we are saying. Proverbs 6:2 says we are snared by the words of our mouths. Many people would refer to this as "self-fulfilling prophecy."

We all hear and see things that create thoughts or ideas in us. But just because we hear or see things doesn't mean we must process them into truth and let them lodge in our hearts. What is to lodge in our hearts is the Word of God; everything else we see or hear must be filtered through the Word of God so that we think godly thoughts, speak godly words, and get godly results.

Wrong thinking and wrong processing can result in wrong believing and thus lead to fear, worry, torment, or any other obstacle Satan wants to throw our way. But right thinking and right processing of what we see and hear can yield right believing and right speaking, which create an atmosphere of faith, filled with life and hope.

FAITH AND THE FIG TREE

Jesus understood the importance of having faith and speaking faith. In Mark 11:22–24 Jesus tells how people of faith are overcomers. Jesus' words are powerful and true: "Have faith in God."

> Have faith in God. For assuredly, I say to you, whoever says
> to this mountain, "Be removed and be cast into the sea," and

does not doubt in his heart, but believes that those things he says will be done, he will have whatever he says. Therefore I say to you, whatever things you ask when you pray, believe that you receive them, and you will have them.

To fully understand the context of these powerful verses about faith, we need to know what happened beginning at Mark 11:12. Jesus spoke to a fig tree (vv. 12–15). He was hungry and approached this tree to find something to eat. Verses 13–14 tell us, "When He came to it, He found nothing but leaves, for it was not the season for figs. In response Jesus said to it, 'Let no one eat fruit from you ever again.'"

For years I did not understand what was wrong in the situation with the fig tree. Mark 11:13 says that figs were not in season, so why was Jesus even looking for figs? And why was He disappointed when He couldn't find one? It really didn't make sense to me.

Greg Lanier from the Gospel Coalition explains this passage in a way that makes sense to me. According to him, the fact that the fig tree had leaves was an indication that it would bear its fruit early (think of the term *early bloomer* or *late bloomer*).[2] When Jesus got closer to it, however, there were no figs. The foliage indicated one thing, but the fruit did not follow. In my words, the figs were in rebellion against the fullness of the leaves. In a sense, the tree said one thing but produced another. And aren't we supposed to be known by our fruit? Faith without works is dead (James 2:17).

Lanier calls what happened with the fig tree "all expectation, no satisfaction." And sometimes the world's way of thinking is contrary to God's way of thinking. In God's kingdom, expectation through faith in God yields results that are not only satisfying; they are miraculous.

When we understand the idea of expectation without satisfaction, the fact that Jesus cursed the fig tree makes sense. When He did so, nothing seemed to happen. Seeing this lack of response from the tree, Jesus went on His way. He did not say, "Watch this." He did not say, "Believe." He did not say, "Don't believe." He simply continued His journey and returned the next day with His disciples to find the fig tree withered.

The disciples seemed shocked that what Jesus had spoken had come to pass. I can't imagine why they didn't believe Him. But they didn't. Peter remembered Jesus' words to the fig tree and said, "Rabbi, look! The fig tree which You cursed has withered away" (Mark 11:21). Jesus didn't respond by saying, "I told you so," or "Why didn't you trust Me?" He simply said, "Have faith in God" (v. 22).

The Lord, who created every living thing, including the fig tree, had the authority to speak to the tree and command it never to produce figs again. When Jesus spoke to the fig tree, He spoke something into the spirit realm with His words. You and I can also speak into the spirit realm with our faith-filled words.

SPEAK GOD'S WORDS

God created this world with His words. He spoke, and what He said became reality (Genesis 1:3, 6, 9, 11, 14, 20, 24, 26, 28, 29). In this way, God showed us an important pattern: believe, speak, see the results.

The same Jesus who spoke to the fig tree was with His Father during the creation of the heavens and the earth (Colossians 1:15–16). He knew how God worked. He knew that God spoke everything into existence with His words. If God can speak something into existence with His words, then why can't God curse something if it rebels against the way it is designed to operate? The split-second Jesus answered that tree and cursed it, it had no choice but to obey the word of God. Jesus did not stand there to watch it because He knew exactly what would happen. He knew by faith that the moment He spoke the word into existence, the tree was required by the laws of God to obey Him.

Against this backdrop, Jesus went on to say, "For assuredly, I say to you, whoever says to this mountain, 'Be removed and be cast into the sea,' and does not doubt in his heart, but believes that those things he says will be done, he will have whatever he says" (Mark 11:23). Then He added, "Whatever things you ask *when you pray,* believe that you receive them, and you will have them" (v. 24, emphasis mine).

Mark 11:24 is a great lesson in faith. Faith does not come into play after the fact. Jesus didn't say we are to believe when we see the manifestation. He didn't tell us to believe when the job is finished or when we have the answer in our hands. Faith is activated the moment we speak the Word of God. The moment we pray is the moment we are to believe.

Jesus continued this lesson about believing and speaking with a critical point: if we want to speak as God tells us to speak, exercise our faith in Him, and see Him work on our behalf, forgiveness is necessary (Mark 11:25). Not optional, but *necessary.* I wrote an entire chapter about it (chapter 10). I just want to remind you again because it is vitally important. When we pray, we are to forgive. Why? Because only forgiveness gives us a clean slate. God can honor that clean slate with no interference between us and our heavenly miracles. If we will simply learn to do things God's way, we can get God's answers and see miracles happen.

THE LAW OF FAITH

When Jesus cursed the fig tree and then said, "Have faith in God" (Mark 11:21–22), He was showing us the power of our words and showing us that our words can be attached to our faith. When we use our words to speak God's Word and then attach our faith to it, the spiritual law of faith begins to work and we begin to see the amazing miracles of God. He promised, "So shall My word be that goes forth out of My mouth: it shall not return to Me void [without producing any effect, useless], but it shall accomplish that which I please and purpose, and it shall prosper in the thing for which I sent it" (Isaiah 55:11 AMPC).

One of several spiritual laws in the Bible is the law of faith, and when we operate in it, using God's words, we receive God's response. When we are in harmony with the Word of God and the will of God, then God watches over His Word to perform it (Jeremiah 1:12).

When Jesus told the disciples to have faith in God, He was teaching a divine principle, using something in the earthly world to explain something of the Spirit. When we speak something into the spirit realm, no matter what we see, what we think, what we feel, or what our opinion is, if God is in it, He says it is supposed to come to pass. We pray, we believe, and in His perfect way, God acts. That's the spiritual law.

God expects us to honor His laws and the way He works. He speaks something into the earth, and it happens, as we read in Genesis 1. If we want God's results, we need to do things God's way. If we will operate as God tells us to operate and do what He tells us to do, we can put ourselves in position to see the results God promises.

HOW ARE YOU USING YOUR WORDS?

Studies show that women speak approximately twenty thousand words per day. While we are utilizing thousands of words per day, my question is, how are we using our words? Are we using them for God's glory, to build His kingdom? Or are we using them against His will and against His Word to create things that do not bring honor and glory to Him?

It is amazing to me that God thinks words are so important that He not only gave us the Word as the Bible, but He also gave us Jesus as the Word clothed in flesh.

Each of us must decide what to do with God's Word and how we will use our words. Regarding God's Word, we would be wise to follow the example of the psalmist who wrote, "Your word I have hidden in my heart, that I might not sin against You" (Psalm 119:11). Regarding our words, let's remember that "out of the abundance of the heart the mouth speaks" (Matthew 12:34) and that the tongue holds the power of life and death (Proverbs 18:21). In addition, Jesus said in Matthew 12:37, "By your words you will be justified, and by your words you will be condemned." The New Living Translation says it this way: "The words you say will either acquit you or condemn you."

Based on these verses, we not only have the scriptural right, but a scriptural responsibility to choose our words and use our words carefully and properly. We can use our words to speak faith, or we can use them to speak doubt, fear, torment, and unbelief. If we speak negative words, should we be surprised if negative things come to pass? And if we speak faith, should we be surprised when miracles manifest?

Our words are vital to the outcome of our lives. When we align our words with God's Word, we can have the biblical privilege of seeing those words come to pass for amazing miracles, signs, and wonders. James 3:4–5 compares the tongue to a tiny rudder that steers a large ship. Because that is true, the words of our mouths can turn our lives around and head us toward smooth sailing, starting right now. Regardless of what you have been through or currently may be going through, you can begin to give God your words and watch amazing miracles start to happen. I'd love for that to happen in your life. My sincere desire is to see you begin to declare the Word of God and reap the amazing miracles of God and begin to experience the fruits of your true worth in God's kingdom.

14

DESTINED FOR VICTORY

Spiritual progress rarely goes unopposed, so don't be surprised as you grow in your sense of worth and value, if the process feels challenging or messy at times. Don't be discouraged if you take one step forward and two steps backward. The most powerful women I have ever known—those who have been most effective in God's kingdom and in life in general—are women who have a keen awareness of how much God loves them, of their identity in Christ, and of how valuable they are to God and to others and what it took to get there.

I've mentioned this before, but when we think of our worth and value, the only way to do it is with humility. Our true worth doesn't come from anything we do, what we look like, how much money is in our bank accounts, where we went to school, what kind of jobs we hold, how accomplished our children are, or anything else. It comes from God alone. We see it in the fact that He sent His Son to die a brutal death on the cross so that all our sins—past, present, and future—are forgiven. If that doesn't help us understand how valuable we are, I'm not sure what would. And because that worth comes from God, we embrace it with gratitude, courage, and humility.

I mention this because some women wonder if embracing their true worth and value is a sign of pride. Nothing could be further from the truth! A woman who humbly recognizes and celebrates her God-given worth is beautiful and powerful. She enjoys herself and her life, and she is a great blessing to the people around her.

God knows how effective a woman who knows her worth can be in His kingdom; and the devil knows it too. I believe that's why Satan tries to stop you from realizing how valuable and significant you are. He does this through the disapproval of other people, through influencing your thoughts about yourself in negative ways, through magnifying your mistakes and failures, and through highlighting flaws or weaknesses—whether they are physical characteristics you'd like to change, emotional struggles, or thought patterns that reinforce things that God's Word does not say about you. Satan will oppose your understanding of your worth and value in other ways, too, so pay attention and be on your guard against him.

As your sense of worth develops, you might experience times when you recognize something wonderful you had not noticed before and times when the enemy flat-out lies to you about yourself. You may have to fight with the good fight of your faith for your worth sometimes, but the fight will be worth it. It's a battle you can win, according to Philippians 4:13, through Christ who gives you the strength.

FIGHT THE GOOD FIGHT

First Timothy 6:12 says we are to "fight the good fight of faith." The spiritual war—not just a cosmic conflict between good and evil, but even the battle for our sense of worth—is a fixed fight spiritually speaking, designed so that we win. Since God has already given us a measure of faith, according to Romans 12:3, we can fight a good fight by using our faith to see our victory.

I've heard people say that it's time to "fight dirty." I laugh when I hear it. "Why fight dirty?" I ask. "Why fight in the flesh when it may not be productive?" Why not fight with mighty spiritual weapons that are backed by the power of God in the name of Jesus? "The weapons of our warfare are not carnal" (meaning, of the flesh), but they are "mighty *in God* for pulling down strongholds" (2 Corinthians 10:4, emphasis mine). That's what I call "fighting on your knees." It's fighting the good fight of faith in prayer.

In addition, I can believe for victory in every battle because I can do all things *through Christ* who gives me the strength to do it (Philippians 4:13). When we do things with balance and in harmony with God's Word and His will, we can call on the "through Christ" part to give us the proper strength to get the job done. So often I wonder why I do things my way rather than first seeking God's ways or methods, which work so much better than mine.

To top it all off, Exodus 14:14 says, "The LORD will fight for you, and you shall hold your peace." As I mentioned earlier, I wrote in the margin of my Bible by this verse, "The Lord will fight for me, and I shall act like a lady." This, of course, isn't an accurate word-for-word translation, but for me, the concept is there.

James 4:7 says we must submit to God, resist the devil, and he will flee from us. We must do our part and fight with our mighty weapons, the good fight of our faith.

Throughout any battle we face, we have the opportunity to worship God. When we praise Him, according to Psalm 22:3, He lives and dwells in our praise. And when God arrives, He comes prepared to do battle on our behalf. Prayer, praise, offerings, worship, faith, our words, and decrees according to His Word are all mighty weapons to pull down strongholds. So don't fight dirty—fight smart! Fight in prayer.

When I urge you to "fight smart," you may be wondering if I'm contradicting what I wrote about the fact that the Lord fights our battles and that all we need to do is hold our peace. Sometimes peace is active. Holding our peace may mean keeping God's Word in our hearts and on our lips. It may mean being diligent to block out fearful or angry thoughts. Holding our peace doesn't mean never doing anything physically, mentally, or in the spiritual realm. It simply means we do not allow our souls to become agitated and upset; it means we stay at rest on the inside, doing whatever God has called us to do while He fights on our behalf. He does indeed fight our battles, but sometimes He asks us to enter into a battle He is fighting through prayer, worship, declaring the Word, and so forth.

With this in mind, let me encourage you to fight spiritually for your identity. Fight for a deep understanding of your worth and value to God. Fight for His purposes to come to pass in your life by using *His* mighty weapons in *His* power and *His* might, and watch *His* results begin to happen.

Sometimes peace is active. Holding our peace doesn't mean never doing anything physically, mentally, or in the spiritual realm.

THE WEAPON OF THE WORD

One of the most powerful spiritual weapons at your disposal as a daughter of God is His Word. Remember that "the just shall live by faith" (Habakkuk 2:4; Romans 1:17), and because of Jesus' sacrifice on the cross, "the just" includes you if you have received Him as your Lord and Savior. How does faith come? By hearing, according to Romans 10:17, "and hearing by the word of God."

The Word of God becomes a mighty spiritual weapon as you hide it in your heart (Psalm 119:11). And then, according to Matthew 12:34, "Out of the abundance of the heart the mouth speaks." When God's Word is in your heart, your words are filled with faith, and you are supposed to walk in the blessings of your faith-filled, Word-based declarations.

"Death and life are in the power of the tongue, and those who love it will eat its fruit" (Proverbs 18:21). Clearly, your words have power. As you take God's Word personally—hiding it in your heart and believing it—and confess it aloud, it becomes a weapon of spiritual warfare. Following are ten Scripture-based confessions you can speak when the enemy tries to rob you of your sense of worth and value.

1. "I am fearfully and wonderfully made." (Psalm 139:14)
2. "God loves me with an everlasting love. He draws me with lovingkindness." (adapted from Jeremiah 31:3)
3. "The Lord rejoices over me with gladness. He quiets me with His love. He rejoices over me with singing." (adapted from Zephaniah 3:17)

4. "God showed His love for me in that while I was still a sinner, Christ died for me." (adapted from Romans 5:8)

5. "Because I am in Christ, I am a new creation. Old things in my life have passed away. I have been made new." (adapted from 2 Corinthians 5:17)

6. "I am strong and courageous. I will not fear or be dismayed, for the Lord my God is with me wherever I go." (adapted from Joshua 1:9)

7. "God, who has begun a good work in me, will bring it to completion." (adapted from Philippians 1:6)

8. "God chose me before the foundation of the world, that I should be holy and blameless before Him in love." (adapted from Ephesians 1:4)

9. "I am God's workmanship, created in Christ Jesus for good works, and I will walk in them." (adapted from Ephesians 2:10)

10. "God has good plans for me, plans to prosper me and not to harm me, plans to give me hope and a future." (adapted from Jeremiah 29:11 NIV)

I'M PRAYING FOR YOU

Another powerful spiritual weapon is prayer, and now that you've reached the end of this book, I'd like to pray for you.

I pray every provision of the Word of God over your life.
I pray you see that many so-called unconventional

things about you are actually gifts from God, gifts that help make you a unique and special woman of worth.

I pray for God to reveal Himself to you in such a way that you know exactly who He is and who you are in Him.

I pray for you to experience the great love and devotion for Jesus that Mary Magdalene, Joanna, and Susanna displayed.

I pray you have the courage of Esther, the wisdom of Deborah, and the great influence of Bathsheba.

I pray you have the ability to be faithful to the task at hand, like Florence Chadwick.

I pray you develop the gracious spirit of Evelyn Roberts, and that, like Evelyn, you will be remembered for your grace and kindness even after your earthly life has ended.

I pray for you to know Jesus as your Savior, Healer, Provider, Waymaker, Deliverer, King of kings, Lord of lords, and, most of all, your Friend.

I pray that you experience and enjoy every day as a gift from God, knowing who you are and keenly aware that you can do all things through Him who gives you strength (Philippians 4:13).

I pray you will grow to expect God to do exceedingly, abundantly, far above anything you could ever ask or imagine (Ephesians 3:20).

And I pray you honestly, genuinely see yourself as God's daughter—a woman of priceless worth and exceptional value.
In Jesus' name, amen.

ACKNOWLEDGMENTS

Beth Ryan: Simply put, without your vision, dedication, insight, constant encouragement, and precious friendship, this book would never have made it into print.

Beth Clark: You are a dear friend and an extraordinary writer who makes words come alive. You found a way to put my heart on the pages of this book.

Janene MacIvor: As my editor, you have not only managed the various pieces of this project with excellence, skill, patience, and prayer, you have cared about the book, its author, and its readers in a most remarkable way.

Stephanie Tresner, Sara Broun, Phoebe Wetherbee, Kristina Juodenas, and the entire HarperCollins design and publishing team: I've come to know you as "the dream team." Thank you for your work, diligence, and encouragement to let women know how really valuable they are. You all are a great joy to work with, talk with, and laugh with.

ACKNOWLEDGMENTS

A very special thank you to *Mike, Jeff, Coleen, Diane, Brian, Penny, Nick, Leanne, and everyone in our "office family"* I've had the privilege of working with for so many years.

Jerry and Carolyn Savelle, Nancy Dufresne, Kellie Copeland, and Joni Lamb: Thank you for being such a blessing to me in so many ways.

Finally, my deepest appreciation and love to my friends and ministry colleagues who have lent their kind words to this book as endorsers. Each of you is inspirational in your love for God and very special to me.

DISCOVERY GUIDE

Dear Woman of Worth,

I trust that your journey through the pages of this book has opened your eyes to your worth and value as a daughter of God. As I think of you, I can sense the Father's heart for you. You are precious to Him and more loved than you can imagine.

My hope for you is that you will continue to discover your worth and value, and that you will become so firmly established in them that nothing and no one will ever again cause you to question them. That's why I have developed this discovery guide. In it you'll find several questions designed to help you think deeper and more personally about the lessons you've learned in this book and to lead you to an even greater understanding of how special you are and how much God loves you.

I don't know about you, but when I think about myself, I can easily identify negative things I don't like, but pointing out the positive aspects of who I am can be challenging. In this discovery guide, I encourage you to consider the questions and frame your answers in ways that will help you identify and recognize your true worth—your true value—chapter by chapter.

You may want to work your way through this discovery

guide alone, or you may want to invite some friends to read this book and work through the discovery guide with you. I believe it can benefit you personally, and that it can be an important resource for groups of women who may want to help and encourage each other to discover how loved and special they are. Whether you use it on your own for personal growth or with a group—or both (you could work through it by yourself and then perhaps lead a group through it), I pray that it will lead you to an amazing and ever-deepening sense of your worth and value to God.

May the Lord bless you today and always!

Love in Christ,
Lindsay

1

WELCOME TO THE UN-CONVENTION

1. Because God has made you special, I have no doubt there are many wonderful, unique things about you. Which of these unconventional characteristics do you like most about yourself?

2. What are your favorite unconventional characteristics in other people—your friends, family members, coworkers, or people you admire from a distance?

3. List three ways you can share your unique characteristics with someone as a blessing to them. For example, I'm a good organizer, and my daughters like it when I organize their closets. One of my daughters is a chef, and I love it when she makes homemade bread for me.

4. Think about your answers to question 2. How can you incorporate something you value in someone else into your life? For example, if you tend to be late and you admire someone who is always on time, what can you learn from that person about

being more punctual? Perhaps you could set your alarm clock five minutes earlier, or maybe you could plan your next day's outfit the night before. Though you are already full of worth and value, you may wish to add more wonderful qualities to your life. Identifying them in others and allowing others to prompt you to develop them can help you while also giving value to those who inspire you.

2

MARY MAGDALENE, JOANNA, AND SUSANNA: THE GUCCI GIRLS

Before you begin answering the questions below, reread Luke 8:1–3.

1. What substance has God given you?

   • For example, you may have enough financial provision to share with others because of a successful job.
   • You may have a strong knowledge of the Bible and the gift of teaching biblical truth to others.
   • Perhaps your living room is large enough to host a prayer meeting for a few friends.
   • Maybe you're a retired teacher who can help children with their homework.
   • Or perhaps you can bake a great casserole.

2. List something you think you can do with what you identified as your substance in question 1.

3. If you could give to God something that you don't yet have, what would it be? (It may be something in your marriage, your children, your home, or a skill or talent you'd like to develop.)

4. Is there someone God is leading you to bless out of your substance? If so, who is it and what can you give to that person? It could be something like prayer, a word of encouragement, a God-given skill or talent, a financial gift, a meal, or hosting a Bible study. In other words, how can you use something God has given you to bless someone else?

5. How can you put your substance to use in ways you've never thought of before? I'm sure the possibilities are endless!

3

IF IT'S BROKEN, FIX IT. IF IT'S NOT, LEAVE IT ALONE. BUT DO NOT GIVE UP.

1. When have you felt someone did a job that you *know* you could have improved upon? What happened, and why do you believe you could have done it better?

2. In a few words, can you identify something you wanted to change but didn't or couldn't—and then you were so glad you didn't change it?

3. Have you ever wanted to quit too soon for a good reason (or even for the silliest reason) but didn't? What happened, and what made you keep going?

4. If you have ever started something but didn't finish it, what good lessons did you learn from it? I really believe I learn a lot of great lessons from things I messed up or didn't finish, so hopefully you'll have a positive answer to this question.

4

BATHSHEBA: THE GOSSIPED GIRL

Since gossip usually uses words to tear down people, let's turn the tables on the devil and use our words to build people up.

1. Do you remember something someone said about you that really made you shine, have hope, or believe in yourself? If so, what was it?

2. Think of three people and of something positive about each one. How can you speak in such a way that you give voice to something about their good qualities or abilities so you properly "spread" praise instead of gossip? For example, my daughter is an anointed singer, so I love to bring that to her attention. Another daughter is a great designer, and I love to tell her she is a creative genius in ways I could never imagine. Another daughter went to culinary school and is also a pastry chef. I love to see her creations and tell her that she should write a cookbook or submit her pastries to a magazine.

3. List words of encouragement that you would like to hear someone say to you. Then say them to yourself. Then, when given the proper opportunity, say them to others. I personally like words such as *kind, creative, funny,* and so forth.

5

IF LIFE WERE A ONE-ACT PLAY . . .

1. First Samuel 30:19 says, "David recovered all." How do these words encourage you and give you hope? If someone asked you to consider practicing words of encouragement and hope about moving into an amazing future in God, what words come to mind?

2. Consider Deuteronomy 30:19 and John 10:10. What can you believe God for to begin a life filled with the blessing and abundance of God?

3. If someone said they would pray for three things to boost you into a life of abundance in God, what would your prayer requests be? Now, take those three things to God and start believing that He hears your prayers and can begin to answer them as He chooses, in His perfect will, and in His perfect timing.

6

ESTHER: MORE THAN JUST A PRETTY FACE

1. For you, what seems like a challenging, perhaps impossible, yet important task? For me, one thing was trying to keep up with and carry out all my father-in-law's creative ideas. It was really amazing to see the ideas he came up with, but it was equally challenging to figure out how to implement them. For you, perhaps it's finding the time to care for young children or aging parents while also taking care of yourself. While these challenges are not the same as Esther's, they may seem overwhelming at times.

2. As you have prayed about what God would have you do, what is the most unusual task you feel He has ever asked you to undertake? Why is it challenging, and why is it important?

3. When God gives me an assignment or an idea, I do two things before anything else: I pray, and I look to His Word. What scriptures can you stand on as you discover and pray about how your God-given assignment or idea unfolds?

4. If you could write a movie script for your own personal "such a time as this" task from God, what would your character be doing in her life right now?

7

DELILAH: QUEEN ESTHER'S TWIN?

When I was in school, I encountered a really unusual teacher who was also a very "difficult" human being. However, strange as it may sound, I learned a great deal from this teacher about the subjects of what not to do and who not to become. With that thought in mind, let's imagine that Delilah was the school-teacher who best taught everyone what not to do.

1. If you had been in Ms. Delilah's class, what might you have noticed about her life that she *could* have used for good, had she chosen to do so? For example, she was dedicated to the mission, she was fearless, and so forth.
2. If Delilah had served God, what could she have done to help Samson instead of defeating him?
3. If you were to privately pray to God for Delilah, how would you pray for her? (I like to remember that when someone prays, anything wonderful from God can happen.)

8

DON'T PUT A COMMA WHERE GOD PUT A PERIOD

1. Can you identify something in the past that you know God has asked you to let go of but you just don't know how to release it or don't want to let go of it? (Keep in mind that this is not a person but rather a thing or an event.)

2. If you can release that "thing," what positive result do you expect to see?

3. Take a moment to read Isaiah 43:18–19. What does this passage mean to you personally, and how does it strengthen you or give you hope?

4. Have you ever reached a point where you had to decide whether the Bible is true or not? What brought you to that point, and why did you make the decision you made?

9

DEBORAH: A WOMAN OF AUTHORITY AND INFLUENCE

1. Do you have a dream, idea, thought, or godly desire about being in a particular leadership role?
2. If yes, do you feel ready for the position?
3. If not, can you identify three basic steps you could take to be prepared for your dream or idea of leadership in the future?
4. As you think and pray about any leadership role to which God may be leading you, have you spent sufficient time in prayer to hear from Him about it? And can you select three scriptures to firmly stand on while you pray it through?

10

BITTER, BETTER, OR SWEET REVENGE?

Question: Should we just skip this and move on?
Answer: Umm, no.

1. Let's make this simple. Ask God to take any bitterness out of your heart.
2. Ask God to reveal to you anyone you need to forgive and to help you forgive that person or those people.
3. Ask God to bless you with His recompense of reward for anything He would like to send your way.

How's that? Short? Sweet but life changing?

11

EVELYN ROBERTS: AN UNFORGETTABLE WOMAN OF KINDNESS

1. Can you identify three women who have influenced your life in similar ways to the ways Evelyn influenced mine?

2. I have been on several podcasts lately, and sometimes I ask the questions and sometimes I answer them. So, if you had a chance to interview the three women you named in question 1 and could ask each woman three questions (the same questions or different ones), what would you ask and why?

3. Concerning each woman in question 1, what three words best describe what you love about her?

4. If you could temporarily switch places with one of the three women, which would it be and why?

5. Rather than switching places with one of the women who has influenced you powerfully in such a positive way, how could you embrace your own worth and celebrate your uniqueness while also incorporating into your life the qualities you most admire in these women?

12

CRAZY, AMAZING MIRACLES

Write down what you would say to me in an interview if we went on a talk show together. Just kidding! However . . .

1. Let's say you were believing God for a miracle and you received it. If someone were to interview you about it, how would you describe what you had believed for, and what would you say happened as God brought it to pass?

2. If someone asked you to believe with them for a miracle, how would you respond?

3. If you were to reach out to Jesus, like the woman in Mark 5:25–34, what unusual miracle would you ask Him for? Do you believe He is able to do that for you?

4. If God were to answer your prayer with what I call a "notable miracle," what would be the first thing you would do? Who would be the first person you would call, and what would you say?

5. Psalm 139:14 says we are "fearfully and wonderfully made." When was the last time someone told you or you told yourself how really wonderful you are to God? Let me say it: "God thinks you are wonderful!" Should I say it again? Okay: "God thinks you are wonderful!" Now will you repeat "God thinks I'm wonderful" at least seven times per day, every day for one month?

13

BECOMING A WOMAN OF FAITH

1. Women reportedly speak approximately twenty thousand words per day. My husband, Richard, says I speak twenty thousand words per day—with gusts of up to thirty thousand words sometimes. So, can you write down at least ten positive words to describe characteristics of some of your favorite people?

2. Use twenty words to describe the things you like best about yourself.

3. Use four sentences to describe your favorite person in the world.

4. Use fifteen meaningful words to describe your goals for yourself in the next few months. These should be actual things that you are currently working on.

5. Now, carefully make a faith-based list of goals you are believing God to help you reach through Christ. Remember Philippians 4:13.

14

DESTINED FOR VICTORY

1. Have you ever thought that discovering and developing a strong sense of your worth to God was prideful? If so, how has this book taught you that celebrating your worth and value with humility is not only biblical, but that it actually honors Him and helps you fulfill His call on your life?

2. Of the Scripture confessions listed in chapter 14, which one (or two) resonates most with you in this current season of your life? Focus on it intensely for several weeks—allowing the speaking of the words to cause them to take root in your heart, transform your thoughts, and change your life.

3. What are some spiritual ways you can fight the good fight of your faith for your sense of worth and destiny while still holding your peace?

4. Thank you for allowing me to pray for you as you finished reading this book. Will you now consider taking that prayer, or a similar one in your own words, and, during your regular

prayer time, spend a few minutes praying for some women in your life? If so, what are their names?

5. Now it's your turn to write a personal statement of faith, hope, worth, and value. I would encourage you to use these three headings or similar ones in your own words. Under each heading, write whatever the Holy Spirit brings to your mind:

- What Positive Things I Believe About Myself According to God's Word (You can find a lot in this book to put under that heading.)
- What I'm Hoping, Praying, and Trusting God For
- I Have True Godly Worth and Value Because . . . (Go ahead and say it all. Brag on yourself. It's okay!)

Scriptures for Reflection

OLD TESTAMENT

"The LORD will fight for you, and you shall hold your peace." (Exodus 14:14)

"Choose for yourselves this day whom you will serve.... But as for me and my house, we will serve the LORD." (Joshua 24:15)

"Who knows whether you have come to the kingdom for such a time as this?" (Esther 4:14)

> Your word I have hidden in my heart,
> That I might not sin against You.
> (Psalm 119:11)

> There are many plans in a man's heart,
> Nevertheless the LORD's counsel—that will
> stand. (Proverbs 19:21)

To everything there is a season,
A time for every purpose under heaven . . .
A time to keep silence,
And a time to speak. (Ecclesiastes 3:1, 7)

[The LORD says,] "For as the heavens are
      higher than the earth,
So are My ways higher than your ways,
And My thoughts than your thoughts." . . .
"So shall My word be that goes forth from
      My mouth;
It shall not return to Me void [without
      producing any effect, useless],
But it shall accomplish what I please,
And it shall prosper in the thing for which I
      sent it." (Isaiah 55:9, 11)

"For I know the plans I have for you," declares the LORD,
"plans to prosper you and not to harm you, plans to give
you hope and a future." (Jeremiah 29:11 NIV)

Through the LORD's mercies we are not
      consumed,
Because His compassions fail not.
They are new every morning;
Great is Your faithfulness. (Lamentations
      3:22–23)

NEW TESTAMENT

The words you say will either acquit you or condemn you. (Matthew 12:37 NLT)

But Jesus looked at them and said to them, "With men this is impossible, but with God all things are possible." (Matthew 19:26)

[Jesus said,] "The thief does not come except to steal, and to kill, and to destroy. I have come that they may have life, and that they may have it more abundantly." (John 10:10)

And do not be conformed to this world, but be transformed by the renewing of your mind, that you may prove what is that good and acceptable and perfect will of God. (Romans 12:2)

We have the mind of Christ. (1 Corinthians 2:16)

For the weapons of our warfare are not carnal but mighty in God for pulling down strongholds, casting down arguments and every high thing that exalts itself against the knowledge of God, *bringing every thought into captivity to the obedience of Christ."* (2 Corinthians 10:4–5, emphasis mine)

Let us not grow weary while doing good, for *in due season* we shall reap if we do not lose heart. (Galatians 6:9, emphasis mine)

That you, being rooted and grounded in love, may have strength to comprehend with all the saints what is the breadth and length and height and depth, and to know the love of Christ that surpasses knowledge, that you may be filled with all the fullness of God. (Ephesians 3:17–19 ESV)

God can do anything, you know—far more than you could ever imagine or guess or request in your wildest dreams! He does it not by pushing us around but by working within us, his Spirit deeply and gently within us. (Ephesians 3:20 THE MESSAGE)

And be ye kind one to another, tenderhearted, forgiving one another, even as God for Christ's sake hath forgiven you. (Ephesians 4:32 KJV)

We do not wrestle against flesh and blood, but against principalities, against powers, against the rulers of the darkness of this age, against spiritual hosts of wickedness in the heavenly places. (Ephesians 6:12)

One thing I do, forgetting those things which are behind and reaching forward to those things which are ahead, I press toward the goal for the prize of the upward call of God in Christ Jesus. (Philippians 3:13–14)

I can do all things through Christ who strengthens me. (Philippians 4:13)

The just shall live by faith. (Hebrews 10:38)

Therefore submit to God. Resist the devil and he will flee from you. (James 4:7)

NOTES

Introduction

1. *Merriam-Webster*, s.v. "substance," accessed August 24, 2021, https://www.merriam-webster.com/dictionary/substance.
2. *Strong's*, G5224.

Chapter 1: Welcome to the Un-convention

1. *Lexico*, s.v. "unconventional," accessed August 22, 2021, https://www.lexico.com/en/definition/unconventional.
2. "Head, Heart, and Gut: How to Use the 3 Brains," Goodnet, August 20, 2020, https://www.goodnet.org/articles/head-heart-gut-how-to-use-3-brains. The article comes from a study published in *SAGE Journals*. "The Three Brains: Why Your Head, Heart, and Gut Sometimes Conflict," Australian Spinal Research Foundation, July 26, 2016, Rick Snyder. "Head, Heart, and Gut: The Three Brains That Control Our Intuition," Invisible Edge, accessed November 16, 2021, https://invisible-edgellc.com/head-heart-gut/. "How Your Head, Heart, and Gut Work Together for a Better You," Sun Warrior, September 10, 2020, https://sunwarrior.com/blogs/health-hub/three-brains-how-your-head-heart-and-gut-work-together.

Chapter 2: Mary Magdalene, Joanna, and Susanna

1. This information can be found in various sources, including Luke 8:3 in the NLT and in the Encyclopedia of the Bible at https://www.biblegateway.com/resources /encyclopedia-of-the-bible/toc.

Chapter 3: If It's Broken, Fix It.

1. Lesley Kennedy, "Titanic by the Numbers: From Construction to Disaster to Discovery," HISTORY, October 30, 2020, https:// www.history.com/news/titanic-facts-construction-passengers -sinking-discovery.

2. "Ketchup Made with Sugar? An Offense Against God for Some Mainers," New England Historical Society, accessed November 16, 2021, https://www.newenglandhistoricalsociety.com /ketchup-made-with-sugar-an-offense-against-god-for-some -mainers/.

3. "Florence Chadwick (USA): 1970 Honor Swimmer," International Swimming Hall of Fame, accessed August 23, 2021, https://ishof.org/Florence-chadwick.html.

4. "Florence Chadwick," Wikipedia, accessed August 23, 2021, https://en.wikipedia.org/wiki/Florence_Chadwick#Biography.

5. "Florence Chadwick," Wikipedia.

Chapter 5: If Life Were a One-Act Play . . .

1. *Lexico*, s.v. "drama," accessed August 24, 2021, https://www .lexico.com/en/definition/drama.

2. Miriam Feinberg Vamosh, "King David's Mother: She Stands for Us," *Miriam Feinberg Vamosh* (blog), May 18, 2018, https:// miriamfeinbergvamosh.com/king-davids-mother-she-stands -for-us/.

3. "Does the Bible Mention David's Mother?" Got Questions, accessed August 24, 2021, https://www.gotquestions.org/David -mother.html.

4. *Lexico*, s.v. "recover," accessed August 22, 2021, https://www.lexico.com/en/definition/recover.

5. *Strong's* H5337.

6. *Strong's* G3406.

7. *Collins*, s.v. "requital," accessed August 24, 2021, https://www.collinsdictionary.com/dictionary/English/requital.

8. *Merriam-Webster*, s.v. "requital," accessed August 24, 2021, https://www.merriam-webster.com/dictionary/requital.

9. *Strong's* G5281.

Chapter 7: Delilah

1. *Lexico*, s.v. "twin," accessed August 24, 2021, https://www.lexico.com/en/definition/twin.

2. *Merriam-Webster*, s.v. "twin," accessed August 24, 2021, https://www.merriam-webster.com/dictionary/twin.

Chapter 8: Don't Put a Comma Where God Put a Period

1. *Merriam-Webster*, s.v. "pulverize," accessed August 24, 2021, https://www.merriam-webster.com/dictionary/pulverize.

2. Vocabulary.com, s.v. "pulverize," accessed August 24, 2021, https://www.vocabulary.com/dictionary/pulverize.

Chapter 10: Bitter, Better, or Sweet Revenge?

1. *Strong's* G3405 and G340.

Chapter 12: Crazy, Amazing Miracles

1. Dictionary.com, s.v. "spit," accessed August 26, 2021, https://www.dictionary.com/browse/spit.

2. Dictionary.com, s.v. "mud," accessed August 26, 2021, https://www.dictionary.com/browse/mud.

3. Dictionary.com, s.v. "miracle," accessed August 26, 2021, https://www.dictionary.com/browse/miracle.

4. Barry Starr, "A Long and Winding DNA," KQED, February 2, 2009, https://www.kqed.org/quest/1219/a-long-and-winding-dna.

Chapter 13: Becoming a Woman of Faith

1. *Strong's* G2531.
2. Greg Lanier, "Why Did Jesus Curse the Fig Tree?," The Gospel Coalition, October 2, 2018, https://www.thegospelcoalition.org/article/jesus-curse-fig-tree/.

About the Author

Lindsay Roberts is a minister, writer, editor, wife, mother, and lifelong student of the Bible. Lindsay hosts the inspirational women's television program *Make Your Day Count*, featuring Bible-based teaching infused with humor, practical application, and insight into the power of God's Word for everyday living. The program includes inspiring stories, special guests, worship music, and delicious recipes. *Make Your Day Count* airs over Victory Network, Love World USA Network, YouTube channel @RichardRobertsORM, Roku channel @Miracles Television, and Miracles Television Mobile app.

In addition, Lindsay cohosts, along with her husband, Richard, *The Place for Miracles*, a half-hour interactive broadcast that reaches millions of viewers worldwide through satellite networks such as Victory Channel, the Word Network, and various other Christian networks and stations. The ministry has received more than 160,000 testimonies from viewers who have reported miracles and answers to prayers through this broadcast outreach.

Lindsay is editor and publisher for Oral Roberts Ministries publications, which includes her *Make Your Day Count* online magazine, as well as books and articles for her husband, Richard, and late father-in-law, Oral Roberts. She is also the author of numerous books, including *Cry for Miracles*, *36 Hours with an Angel*, *Overcoming Stress*, the 31-day devotionals *Read & Pray & Then Obey* and *Read & Pray & Then Obey Volume 2*, and many more.

Lindsay is a sought-after speaker at churches, women's conferences, and online services, where she ministers and encourages men and women with the message of hope and life from God's Word.